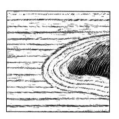

The Art of
Setting
Stones

& Other Writings from the Japanese Garden

MARC PETER KEANE

Stone Bridge Press • Berkeley, California

Published by
STONE BRIDGE PRESS
P. O. Box 8208, Berkeley, CA 94707
sbp@stonebridge.com • www.stonebridge.com

Printed in the United States of America.

10 9 8 7 6 5 4

LIBRARY OF CONGRESS CATALOGING-IN-PUBLICATION DATA
Keane, Marc P. (Marc Peter)
            The art of setting stones : & other writings from
    the Japanese garden / Marc Peter Keane
                                        p. cm.
        ISBN 978-1-880656-70-9
        1. Gardens—Japan—Kyoto—Anecdotes. 2. Gardening—Japan—
        Kyoto—Anecdotes. 3. Keane,
        Marc P. (Marc Peter). I. Title.

        SB455 .K36 2002
        712'.0952—dc21
        2002026819

FOR MOMOKO

CONTENTS

INTRODUCTION

A S PEOPLE LIVE ON THE LAND, AS THEY BUILD THEIR HOMES AND temples, towns and cities, they form the world around them into the shape of their philosophies. Their social structures and spiritual mindsets take physical form—as mass and space, material and void—and become the world they live in. This must be true in all places. I have found it to be true in Kyoto.

The jumble of modern Kyoto expresses the disparate sentiments of its present residents as they struggle with the rapid installation of non-native technology and culture. That struggle has left the city with the gawky awkwardness and blemishes of adolescence, but Kyoto has more than that to offer. Much more. To find it, however, you must know where to look: places like the gardens, shrines and temples, and narrow, earth-walled alleyways. It is there that a deeper current of Kyoto's culture has been crystallized and given form, and it is there we can return to come in touch with the myriad forces that originally caused those places to be as they are—nature, economy, geomancy, religion. The nice thing is, you don't really need to study to understand them. You just have to be there. The places speak for themselves.

I've lived in this city for just shy of two decades and spent more than my fair share of time in those places. The more they spoke, the more I felt I should record what they were saying. So that's what I did. The first two of those records, "Boundaries" and "Currents," were published in 1999 in issues 39 and 42 of the quarterly magazine *Kyoto Journal*. The others were written thereafter and are published here for the first time.

If you happen to visit Kyoto you will find the city as a whole differs in quality from the descriptions herein. That is because I have purposefully focused on those places in Kyoto that please the mind and nurture the soul. If you look, however, you can still find many places such as I describe, at times well-known and packed with busy tourists, more often secreted away and indescribably still. But, you will not find precisely the places I describe. They are, in fact, mosaics of my memories and exist only within these pages. What I have written might well be considered a guidebook but not one to actual places. Rather it is a general guide to certain basic principles that the gardens, temples, and shrines of Kyoto articulate, and to what we can gain from listening to them.

❀   ❀   ❀

And a final note of thanks, to Ken Rodgers, for streamlining the flow.

M. P. KEANE
abiding an early cherry tide
March 2002, Kyoto

all things are symbolic
by their very nature

and all talk of something
beyond themselves

THOMAS MERTON

The illustrations in this book were done on black clayboard by the author, whittling away the cold evenings at his hori-kotatsu, during the late Autumn and Winter of 2000.

CURRENTS

NORTH OF KYOTO, LOW MOUNTAINS EXTEND IN RANKS THAT CON-tinue uninterrupted to the sea. Except for narrow strips of open flatland in the valleys, cleared sometime in the distant past for rice fields and hamlets, the mountains are covered by thick coniferous forests and in places an older, primordial vegetation. The passing wind filters down through the leafy canopy and there, amid endless shadows, it moistens and cools, grows heavy, and begins to flow ever so slowly down the mountainsides toward the valleys below, slipping gently through scattered bracken and piles of fallen branches edged with moss.

At the base of one of those mountains, lying in the path of such a cooling breeze, is a small walled garden. The breeze enters, carrying in the scent of the forest and at times a fine mist that makes its flow perceptible—just barely and for a brief moment. Then the mist dissolves and only the trembling of slender bamboo leaves reveals the currents in the air. Nearing the house, the air slows and meanders in random spirals, pooling above the moss, among the trunks of the garden trees. In cycles it gusts, subsides, then grows stronger again, and though the rhythm of these subtle surges is neither uniform nor constant, somehow they suggest a quiet breathing.

In the garden, just beyond reach of where I sit on the veran-da, is a round camellia tree covered with large, oval flower buds, pointed and green, protruding above a bed of dark, glossy leaves. The buds are fat like silkworm cocoons ready to burst, and one in particular seems right on the verge of opening, the dark-green sheath that wraps the flower eased open just enough to reveal a glimpse of pink within. It intrigues me and I wait patiently for the moment it will open, hoping I'll be watching when it does. It's not the flower I'm interested in, although I'm sure it will be beautiful. No, it's the moment that I await, the instant of opening, when the bud, fed to satisfaction on the nectar of the tree, will suddenly transform and blossom.

For the past two days I have been staying with a poet who lives here on the outskirts of Kyoto. The garden is to the rear of his old wooden house, just where the slope of the mountain levels to the valley floor. A quiet place, the garden has more in common with the mellow rhythms of the forest than the urgency of the nearby city, and the earthen wall that surrounds it is only partially successful at dividing it from the woods beyond. The breeze, of course, ignores all such borders; a large camphor tree and a stand of tall bamboo arch over the garden from outside the wall, casting pools of shade that foster a velvet moss; a small brook winds under the wall and murmurs quietly past me, half-hidden by azaleas and tufts of ferns.

Suddenly the sound of clattering plates comes from the next room. My host, Yukio, now in his mid-seventies, must be getting up and about. He's a character, endearingly old-fashioned. More often than not he strolls about in wooden sandals and kimono, sporting a dapper, wide-brimmed linen hat in the turn-of-the-century Taisho style. Like his clothes, his house is traditionally appointed, except for the veranda where I now sit and on which he has set two low rattan chairs and a small table. He enjoys nothing more than entertaining his guests there, within arm's reach of the garden.

Called an *engawa*, the veranda is less than a meter wide, floored with long, slim planks of fine-grained wood now smooth and dark from years of use. It serves as both a corridor connecting the rooms of the house and as a place from which to enjoy the garden. Sitting here alone today, sipping pale green tea, I watch the morning light fall softly over the budding camellia, reflecting on when I last saw the garden—how then, as now, it seemed to capture a moment of time.

It was December last, at the funeral for Yukio's wife, Chizuru. A cold day, but not bitterly so, perhaps only because the house

was so full of guests kneeling shoulder to shoulder on the tatami, facing an altar that had been set up for the funeral at the front of the room. A black-and-white photo of Chizuru taken some years earlier was set in the center, surrounded by flowers and delicate gilded ornaments. By the altar, a priest knelt reciting sutras, accompanying his rhythmic chants by striking a hollow wooden gong, a sound that both mesmerized and awakened. From my seat at the back of the room, I watched him over rows of black mourning suits, each drawn in a loose curve across a somber back.

In front of the altar was a low table on which was set a small ceramic urn half-filled with fine ash and a few glowing embers. The guests each added three pinches of powdered incense as they took turns to approach the altar to pray, and as the powder fell onto the glowing coals, wisps of pale smoke rose quickly and disappeared. The woody scent pervaded the house: sweet, pungent, somewhat medicinal, recalling ancient temple halls and the darkly gilded Buddhas hidden amid their perpetual shadows.

Off to the right, past the mourners, beyond the veranda, the garden lay covered by a layer of new snow. The sun was muted by dark gray clouds, the garden shadowless, and so it appeared no more real than an ink painting—flat and layered, having depth but no volume. I rose to take my turn at the altar, gave incense and prayer, then turned to see Chizuru in her coffin, pausing briefly for a last look at her white face shrouded in crisp linen. Returning to my place on the tatami, I glanced outside and was struck by how the garden, too, seemed exceptionally pale and peaceful. I thought it couldn't have been a more beautiful time for her funeral, and that Chizuru, as an artist, would have agreed.

The tall bamboos beyond the garden wall were bent over under the weight of the snow, lending the garden an air of sadness. There was, as well, a sense of closure in the garden that seemed appropriate. All the leaves were gone from the maples, and the bushclovers, which had just a short while earlier filled the garden with their soft autumn colors, were now cut back to the point where only stiff clusters of barren stems stuck out from beneath the cover of snow. Gone, too, were the bell crickets whose metallic chirping had echoed in the garden on cool autumn nights, their husks now silent, cold, and brittle beneath the garden's white mantle.

As I watched, it began to snow, large flakes descending more slowly than gravity should allow, floating straight down out of a gray windless sky and gathering on the ground without making a sound. The snow fell earthward in endless lines; yet from where I sat inside, it felt instead as if we were rising, the room and garden together ascending through icy clouds to heaven.

The winter garden and the funeral were perfectly aligned, a time of ending. Yet Chizuru believed fervently in reincarnation, the continuation of souls beyond death in another time and space. It was something we had talked about late into the night on more than one occasion, with me usually playing devil's advocate, prodding the conversation forward with my disbelief.

Watching the frozen garden, I began to feel differently. Couldn't it be, even as the garden remained dormant beneath the snow awaiting the warmth of spring—as the buds of next year's growth, even then in coldest winter, set themselves in incalculable numbers; as the sap that would fuel that growth, gathered and pooled in deep-rooted reserves—that Chizuru's soul was somewhere, in a time or a space intangible, gathering and pooling in preparation for a Spring unknown to us? If the cycles of time that are inherent in the garden are simply an expression of fundamental principles of nature, and if those same principles are expressed in all of nature's myriad forms, then why not in life itself?

On the day of her funeral there was a small photo of Chizuru in the entry hall, a sepia print, somewhat faded at the edges. It showed her dressed in a loose summer yukata, pregnant with her first child, sitting on the *engawa*, her legs dangling over the edge into the garden. She seemed so young in the picture, as did the garden. The photo must have been taken just after she married Yukio and they built the house, and I realized in seeing it that Chizuru's life for the last fifty years had been intertwined with this house—had been in time with this garden. I remember Yukio telling me that he had planted a tree each time one of his children was born: a pine for his eldest son, a plum for the first girl; the others I don't recall. The children are grown now, as are the trees. I wonder what they think when they look into the garden and see a living marker of their time on earth? When I was young, perhaps just one or two, my father stuck a willow twig in the ground in our backyard, and it took root. By the time I was old enough to climb, the willow was big enough to hold me, and by the time I got too old for those things, the willow had grown too big to climb

anyway. For my part, that willow has always seemed both a marker of time and a childhood friend.

❀   ❀   ❀

The camellia bud remains unopened, so I look about the garden
for other changes. There's something about the garden today that
makes it appear unusually solid, voluptuous, and tangible, not
the two-dimensional thing it was during Chizuru's funeral. The
pines are lush with dark needles, the moss deep and verdant,
hummocked into miniature hills; even the shadows of the gray,
lichened stones hug the ground like patches of thick, dark carpet.
It rained heavily yesterday, and the neatly trimmed plants have
swelled luxuriantly. There is also something about the rain-
washed air, a clarity of light and shadow, that makes the garden
seem more three-dimensional.

Into that solidity, a plum tree casts its spent blossoms. It
had been flowering brilliantly for a few days but yesterday's rain
and today's warmth have pushed the flowers toward the verge of
decay. The tiny fibrous tendrils that tie the petals to their stems
have loosened to the point where the slightest breeze detaches
them. Each time the wind gusts, a puff of pink-white dots gushes
like confetti, floats briefly on the current of air, drifts, then pools
neatly on the moss around the bases of trees and the garden
rocks. Such a short time between when the new buds open and
when the flowers fall. They never even seem to fade but simply
cast off into the wind—so utterly carefree. If the pines and stones
are solid, then the cascades of plum blossoms are liquid, and
when they scatter, the garden seems more river than terra firma.

Time, too, is liquid. It flows like the brook that murmurs in from the forest and, like that brook, it moves continuously but not consistently. As the brook sometimes eddies and gathers in slowly spiraling pools that still to the point of silence, so too there is a time that passes slowly, in a measured, unhastened way. And as there are places where water surges forward, slipping fast and smooth in dark, glassy sheets between rounded boulders or stumbling white and ragged over rocky stretches, so too is there a kind of time that hurries along, passes all too quickly, and is gone.

The sun, having risen above the grove of bamboo, angles into the veranda and warms my legs, illuminating the page of a book that lies open on the table. The book is a Japanese commentary on the *I Ching*, an ancient Chinese classic that delves into the mysteries of the physical world. The *I Ching* has been called the *Book of Changes*, a name that reveals the central theme of the text: change is no more than the outward manifestation of time. Time itself cannot be perceived as an entity; instead, it is understood in the form of changes in the physical world that mark its passage, the way trembling leaves reveal a passing breeze. I have brought the commentary with me in hope that it will prove useful as a guide to change, and thus to time, in the garden. The sunlight highlights a section of the text I have been mulling over that contains two words, *hen* and *fuhen*, mutability and permanence, which express the dual nature of time.

The wind scatters more pink across the dark green moss. Plum blossoms—the consummate symbol of mutability in Japan. My favorite, though, is another, what the Japanese call *shinryoku*, the new green of spring. The transience of new leaves is not as noticeable as plum blossoms because, unlike the flowers, the leaves do not fall to mark the end of their youth. They remain on the tree and age; but with no less clarity, there is a time when their newness passes. At first a tender translucent green, incandescent as lapis lazuli, their color deepens and mellows as the leaves turn hard and protective. Like the porcelain clarity of a baby's skin that turns opaque with time, the leaves lose their virginal hue; their moment is gone. When the maple leaves come out in another month or so there will be a brief time—a week or a day, perhaps no more than an hour—when the color of the garden verges on electric; after that it will just be green.

The breeze lofts again; a tiny bug that has been fluttering in the bushes near the veranda drifts over toward me. It alights briefly on the table then flits away, one of those lithe spring apparitions whose winged life spans only a few days—so short-lived it must view plum blossoms as eternal while we mourn their brevity. The cadence of time is not fixed by any timepiece, but rather is based on the perceptions of the observer. The touchstone against which we measure time is the human condition— the length of our life span, the number of our waking hours, the meter of our breaths and heartbeats. I imagine there are some rhythms in the garden so quick, so minute in their fluctuation, that they remain beyond the limit of our perception, the way infrared light does. And then there are rhythms, like those of plum blossoms, that we can perceive but because in comparison to our lives are so brief we term them ephemeral, evanescent. Plum blossoms and new green leaves; bamboo growing in a week-long panic from shoot to tree; a haze of moss-green that appears on the ground only briefly just after a rain and then disappears; the scent of *kinmokusei* blossoms that give but a week's pleasure. But there are also changes that are not brief.

And so, like a river that flows at different speeds, there are many different currents of time within the garden. If plum blossoms and new leaves signify brevity, then the depth of time, as can only be revealed at a slower meter, is manifest elsewhere: in the patina of old clay walls, soft-green edging on their weathered brown scars; in the luster of granite paving stones polished smooth by the touch of passing feet; in the thick trunk and massive crown of the camphor tree that records the passage of centuries.

The wind picks up momentarily and my eye is caught by supple waving branches: a young silk tree at the east side of the garden. In Japan it is called the "sleeping tree," *nemunoki*, because of the way its fernlike leaves fold up each evening, closing for the night as if going to sleep. At dawn the morning light urges them open again. The silk tree reminds me that the cadence of time in the garden is not just linear—not just a matter of being slow or fast—it is also cyclical. It shows in the leaves of the silk tree; in myriad shadows that play across the mossy floor of the garden from west to east, and repeat, patterned anew, each day; in unfolding seasons that eventually recur. The *I Ching* commentaries make an interesting comment on seasons: although they appear to be the epitome of change—one replacing the other ad infinitum—by annually returning to the point from which they started, they also express consistency. Change and continuity, it is written, are not mutually exclusive.

But even though the regenerative aspect of time expresses consistency or permanence, in the garden the close of each cycle also reveals new aspects—the plants are larger, the earthen walls a little more weathered, the ground somewhat mossier. The year returns in a cycle, spring to spring, fall to fall, but it is not exactly the same garden that greets the return.

Some day I would like to map that flow of time. I would draw it in fine gold lines on a large sheet of dark indigo paper the way the ancients used to write their sutras, one line for each thing in the garden: pine, maple, rock, brook, garden wall. Each would trace a spiral path, circling back upon itself to reflect the cyclical changes of the seasons, but also moving forward across the page expressing the changes inherent in linear time. A map of time in the garden would develop that way: dizzy spirals, thousands of them, twisted around each other, intersecting, falling away, regrouping—in the end, mazelike scribbles, incomprehensible but to the mind of God.

Although cycles of time can express permanence, in the garden the clearest symbol of eternity is the rock, an image of the mountain. Stones have been seen as icons of mountains since ancient times, like those that were used to represent Mount Sumeru, which the Buddhist and Hindu religions propose to be the center of the universe. Sumeru is described in legend as being immobile, unchanging, the one fixed element in the Great Flux. Rocks are of course not immutable; they change, but at a pace so slow that, when compared to our lives, they do seem eternal. In Yukio's garden there is one rock set apart, somewhat higher than the others, loosely pyramidal, with outward sloping sides. It too is a symbol of an eternal mountain, a reference against which to measure oneself. It doesn't matter that it is not actually eternal, because it is simply an icon representing an ideal, a belief in something that cannot be . . . that which is without time.

These patterns of time are in the garden and yet they are also in the wild. Plum trees flower there just as readily, streams cross meadows with as many twists and bends, and granite mountains dwarf any garden rock. The difference between the wild and a garden is that the images of time in the garden are there because we put them there. In the same way we capture a moment of time when we write a poem or brush ink to paper, we plant a plum in the garden to revel in the beauty inherent in the brevity of life, or we set a rock there to give ourselves a glimmer of hope that there may be in this transient world things that are eternal. Although wild nature has the potential to convey the same meanings, gardens do so more succinctly. To some degree this may be because gardens are often physically closer to our lives and thus more accessible, but the eloquence of the garden also stems from the fact that it is not wild, that in having been created by human hands, it is more like us, more reflective of our mentality.

A faint woody scent comes on the breeze. Yukio has been tending the small altar in the next room and must have lit some incense. Smelling it, I recall Chizuru's funeral, when everything was clothed in white and the garden harbored the very moment of a death in the silence of its own sleep—so different from the garden today, flush with new life. Looking back at the camellia, I see that the flower has opened. I missed it, but I'm not surprised. These moments are elusive.

The soft, pink flower pushes outward, bathed in sunlight, and I recall a day long ago, a moment not dissimilar. Coming home from work, my young son ran to greet me out of the shadows of our house. As he stepped out into the warm afternoon light, I saw to my surprise an older child than I anticipated. Just a flash—the strength with which he held his head, the tautness of the skin around his eyes. I found myself facing a boy, not a baby, and simply couldn't remember when that change had happened. The boy, like the flower—it is not the process of their changing but the realization of their having changed that impresses the mind because it is in that moment we sense time most clearly.

Yukio calls from the next room. I close the book on the table and sip the last drops from my cup, taking a few tea leaves with it. They taste green, like grass. I should go see what he wants, but I linger at the garden's side. The breeze lifts and falls in a sigh, nudging the plum blossoms that lie in drifts like pink dunes against the garden stones. The brevity of blossoms, the timelessness of stones—perhaps we enjoy nature's rhythms in our gardens because they remind us of the rhythms of our own lives. In the corners of the garden that are most fragile and most constant; in the vast, complex wheel of the seasons; in just one small, nascent blossom—there is a poem of time in which we read our histories and sense by that our futures.

BOUNDARIES

I HAVE BEEN SITTING IN THIS OLD TEMPLE FOR OVER AN HOUR, LOOK-ing out at the garden from a room that is a model of planar geometry expressed in subtle shades of sepia: clay-plastered walls sectioned neatly by posts and beams, modular tatami mats, and grid-patterned paper doors. In contrast, the garden is a verdant transcendence of mathematics. It's early spring; the world seems to tremble, everything emergent, being born anew. The camellias off to the side of the garden are full blown, dropping not petal by petal but in their entirety, clumping like clotted blood around the base of the trees.

In the garden there is a pond, neatly tucked between the temple and the hillside beyond. It reminds me of a pearl of water caught in the hollow of a lotus leaf, glistening like liquid mercury—pure as the soul of Buddha. A dense forest encompasses the rear of the pond, hiding it in shadow, but off to the right the trees become more sparse, giving way to a moss-covered yard in which stands an old prayer hall, weathered and noble. The trees in the yard, with more space between them than those in the forest, have filled out majestically and carry their crowns high above the moss. From where I sit, inside the temple hall, the vertical lines of the posts along the veranda echo the straight, brown, cedar trunks in the yard beyond. Two forests: one live, one lumbered.

Through the trees that ring the pond the sky shows in mov-ing patches of blue and white. Clouds passing overhead let sun-light through intermittently, at times strong then fading, rising again, and as the landscape brightens and dulls it seems to twist and bend, expanding and contracting into pools of light and shadow. Now the sun is out and a soft light filters down through layers of translucent new maple leaves to the smooth surface of the pond, reflecting a cool pale green on the trees and boulders at the water's edge. Waves of light ripple off the water, shimmer up the stones, the trunks and branches of the trees, rising in endless waves as if returning to the sun. A small brown warbler, an *uguisu*, flits back and forth among the branches, restless with nervous energy.

Everything about this place seems to belong here. The water that slips out from the shadows of the forested hillside at the back of the pond and pools before running on to the river below. The temple that sits so comfortably by the pond, shaded by the spreading cover of old trees. The gravel path leading out to the prayer hall, meandering to avoid tree roots as it winds through the carpet of moss. All of these seem not to be separate elements fitted together in one place, but rather elements that are very much of the place. Born of it, nurtured by it, at one with it. Complete.

What keeps recurring in my mind, and what has kept me here in this chilly hall for the last hour, is the question of where the mountain ends and where the garden begins. What here is natural and what man-made? Surely the path through the moss was built, and the gray granite lantern in the shadows of the maples by the back of the pond was set there, no doubt about that. But what about the smooth boulder the lantern rests on, or the maple that arches gracefully above it, or the pond itself? Were these set out by design or have they always been here? The whole appears seamlessly connected—mountain, pond, mossy yard, and temple, too—and somewhere in that unity I feel lies the mystery of the garden.

The desire to understand that integrity has set me hunting for the boundaries of the garden, but it occurs to me now that, as is so often the case, the difficulty in finding the answer is that the question is all wrong. What I am puzzling over is not what is natural and what man-made, but "What is nature?" Concealed in that question is the essence of the garden.

What is nature? If common usage of the word is taken as its definition, nature would be that which occurs without the impetus of the human hand or exists free from its control. After all, we consider the words "natural" and "man-made" to be opposites, defining each other in the negative. Yet, the moment we accept that definition, we separate ourselves from nature, placing ourselves outside looking in, which we are not. However much we may wish to set ourselves apart by defining a hierarchy of living things, with us conveniently on top, there is no separation. We are integral to the whole.

There are some rare moments in our lives when that unity appears so clearly it stuns as it pleases, like the first gulp of air after a long dive. I felt it in Canada one night canoeing on a pond after a thunderstorm. The air was crystalline, cleansed by the rain. Shards of lightning crackled off in the distance as the last black clouds eased over toward the horizon, and in the ensuing calm an ocean of stars flowed out into an ink-black sky and cast themselves across the glassy surface of the water. Stars above, stars below, and a boy gliding silently through them, paddling through the universe. I have felt it floating motionless on the surface of the warm sea off Hawaii, bobbing gently, each breath in synchrony with the rhythms of the surf as if the waves were breathing for me. I feel like it might happen here and now, and just the thought sends shivers along the skin of my back.

I have felt the unity, but not often; those moments are rare and magical. And I also see that people do things that suggest we are separate from nature, "unnatural" things that appear to make us different from other species. We murder our own kind, wage cruel and calculated wars. But if cold-bloodedness is proof of our unnaturalism, consider for a moment the callous acts of some other species. Lions are known to consume their own off-spring, inexplicably, still wet and clinging at the moment of birth. Dominant males among social primates will kill the young of others to free their mothers for their own seed. Female praying mantises devour their mates while copulating, crunching away from head on down, even as the remains of the hapless males continue to pump away at procreation. If we look objectively at the world, without beginning our inquiry with the predeter-mined bias of a man/nature division, the question that immedi-ately comes to mind is: "Are we so different?"

A break in the clouds momentarily highlights the valley be-yond the prayer hall. From end to end it is filled with boxlike houses and a maze of powerlines. Not a single tree in sight. The light fades again and the valley recedes, leaving me with an image of ugliness, cold and suddenly sad. Perhaps just this sort of wan-ton destruction of the environment for selfish purposes is the de-ciding factor that sets us apart from the rest of the ecosystem. We harvest more than we return, cauterize our rivers with concrete, despoil our land with toxic waste. But even as I think this I am re-minded of North American beavers, flooding entire valleys to build their homes and in the process drowning neighbors by the thousands in their earthy burrows. Trees, too, die by the acre, their roots submerged and suffocated. The beavers, who build their houses of these trees, fell them and then use the very pond

35

that killed them to float the trunks where they wish. Admirably efficient selfishness. Are we so different? We kill for selfish purposes; we lay our own backyard to waste.

The little brown warbler has been flitting between the trees in the forest. It flies out of the trees into the streaked light by the pond, hides briefly in a hedge by the temple hall, then back to the forest, quick across the water, lost in the shadows and gone. The uguisu sees no boundary: forest canopy and garden hedge are equally home. I watch as it emerges again and crosses over to the old prayer hall, which sits well above the ground on a platform of stone, its roof held high by twelve massive wooden columns. A sense of pride is expressed in its erect posture, and one of grace in the upward sweeping lines of the roof, supported by a wondrously complex puzzle of interlocking wooden brackets. The temple eloquently expresses the spiritual desires of the priest who commissioned it; the harmonic balance of the whole remains as a tribute to human achievement.

So perhaps it is not our destructive capacity so much as our noble acts, our higher achievements in science and art, like the graceful prayer hall, that separate us from the rest of nature. But are we really that advanced? Does our architecture in any way but size, for instance, surpass the gossamer, crystalline webs of spiders? The microscopic intricacy of their silken threads, which apparently are actually sheathed cables of pleated keratin, is well beyond the present capabilities of human science to explain let alone reproduce, and although arachnids may not be adept at a wide range of skills, when it comes to construction detailing, their genius is downright humbling. One such creature, all black and yellow and needle legs, inhabits my front garden. Somehow, in the space between the fir tree and the huge gardenia that frame the entry walk, she finds just the right twigs to anchor her threads, and though I don't imagine she can see well enough to design the whole from afar, nonetheless, her master planning is impeccable.

Despite prolific examples like these of the overwhelming complexity of the organic world, we still tend to pride ourselves that the sophistication of our technology shows us to be not just one of the multitude of species, but in a class by ourselves. And yet, what if we compare human achievement with that of other species; for instance, compare a nuclear reactor with a leaf—both producers of energy. By applying the greatest concentration of intellect and capital currently available we can build reactors and make them work, barely. Can anyone build a leaf? Music is another of our great accomplishments, but surely none of the astounding variety of instruments we have invented emits a sound more moving and potent than the dulcet call of the little brown uguisu, darting now among the trees—a melodious blur. Are we so different? We build, we sing.

At the end of the room is a *tokonoma*, a small alcove in which artwork is displayed. Its floor is a single panel of beautifully grained wood; the walls are clay. Shadows gather about the back of the recessed space but a soft light from the garden casts across the front, illuminating a rough earthenware vase in which stands a single stem of tree peony. The twisted, gray branch is tipped with a feathery red bud the size of a quail egg, already beginning to open. A row of more peonies grows along the veranda, echoing the single bud in the room, hundreds of russet spots that flit this way and that as if dabbed onto the stems in quick strokes.

The changing light shifts within the bare branches catching the uguisu flitting within. It darts back out, across the pond into the trees above the waterfalls disappearing suddenly upon entering the shadows as if switched off. Peonies in vases, peonies in ground; forests of pillars and forests of trees. Inside and out stitched together with gossamer threads of intimation and mood. Art, architecture, garden, mountain—the whole conversing, interrelated if not indivisible.

Of course the world is divisible, and so much the better. What strange slurry would result if all the parts dissolved one into the other? We cannot do so, we should not, even though some species almost have, like the lichen that patterns the garden stones with circular gray blooms. I could go over and touch them, peer down at the thin flaky disks with magnifier in hand and still never see the odd truth: that lichen is not a single, separate thing, but two—algae and fungus—living together so closely as to be indiscernible. Blue-green algae offers carbohydrates to the fungal host; the fungus in return provides shelter, a solid structure the algae doesn't have. It's a relationship that works, famously. The two have lasted together, in one form or another, since the early Devonian period, four hundred million years ago. But symbiotic relationships this immediate are rare, and so much the better. We have our own forms for a reason.

We are integral to nature, not outside looking in, but neither are we intended to be wholly unified, lying close with lion and sheep in a pastoral valley. That's too cozy. In some ways we are symbiotic—like lichen though not as rarefied—living with other species in relationships based on mutual dependency and support. Yet we are also predators, and at times parasites, taking from our environment without returning the favor. We prey on some, share with others; give a little, take a little. Whether this is a good thing or not all comes down to a question of balance, and balance is where we fail: we are not as extreme in our symbiotism as lichen, but we push parasitism to the limit.

Para means "beside" and *site* "food"; the original meaning of the word was "one who eats at another's table." Some parasites are just annoying guests who grab from your table, like the spider mites in your hair, so minuscule you're not even aware of them. Others cause serious injury to their host, some fatally. The stunning thing in all of this is that some parasites actually die with the host they kill. Can it be so? That life can be ingrained with such reckless abandon? When a parasite unwittingly destroys itself with its host it really should be called an "autosite" because it's feeding at its own table, on *itself*, and therein lies the fundamental debate. We need not ask if we are part of nature or not; we've been dealt in from the start. And it's not a question of whether or not we should fall into a perfect symbiosis with all of nature, like hands entwined in prayer. That is as unattainable as it is undesirable. The question is, are we autosites, parasitic to the point that we are eating away at ourselves? We may not be lichen, but are we locusts?

Locusts turn out to be simply grasshoppers under stress. Crowded beyond a certain genetically triggered limit, they clump and mass on the dusty savannah, restless, clattering madly while they metamorphose into their migratory form. Their mandibles grow, wings expand, and body color heightens to the delirious. Exhilarated by their own energy, they swarm, darkening the sky. Spreading across the land in numbers that have been calculated in the billions they consume everything in their path until, having recklessly eradicated their own source of life, they die, en masse.

We probably reached our inbred limit long ago; its hard to tell, we don't color like locusts, but our ancestors have been migratory for the last million years. And delirious. We spread out and, about ten thousand years ago, we too started really darkening the land, consuming everything in our path. The old story.

It won't matter a tick to nature if we blow it. In fact, like locusts, even if we do self-destruct, we'll more than likely rebound in time, in some form or other. Total and absolute self-annihilation is unlikely, but that's not a real selling point for wanton recklessness. Who wants to be among the unlucky ninety-nine percent?

We live in a perpetual repetition of life and death—consuming and being consumed—a basic truth as applicable to subatomic particles as it is to galaxies. Hindus call it *samsara*; to Japanese it's *rinne*, the Great Wheel turning. Scientists calculate the sums of the parts and call it ecology; ecological visionaries synthesize those sums into Gaia, a self-regulating living entity that covers and interpenetrates the entire planet.

I look into the garden and see fragile edges blurring into a mountain. The sunlight is strong; the moss boundless. Time coats everything. Lost in this country temple, lost here in thought, lost in a dream of another time and place, I feel that if I sit any longer I too will succumb to the patina and be rooted in this hall forever, facing the pond and courtyard with its sunlight that never lights the scene the same way twice.

I look outside again and something happens, at once strange

and wonderful. I take a deep breath to enjoy the scent of the forest and the universe inhales with me. Suddenly, and with great force, the air expands. The shimmering forest on the other side of the pond snaps into focus, each flickering leaf a story, its countless watery cells rushing as audibly as the waterfall. The tatami runs cool and smooth beneath my fingers. A sweet scent beckons, barely apprehensible. Witchhazel flowers, this late in the season? The uguisu cries, sharp and utterly clear like a Noh master's drum. Not a thing has changed, not a drop, not a photon, and yet I am new. Now not on the floor—part of it. Not in the temple—I am the temple, and I am immensely old; I have been here forever. I am the mountain and the pond, I know the air and the water and the trees by name. I am them. The uguisu flies over, settles lightly in my branches and sings.

41

I wish this feeling would last for eternity. I flow within the garden, filling the space between the trees and temple like air, listening to the echoes of stories that linger there. The mountain begets the temple, its ancient trees becoming the wooden frame, its clay earth the sepia walls. The pond water speaks of oceans it had passed through, of rising in vortices through electric thunderheads, of settling down as mist caressing the forest nearby. And sudden beams of sunlight flash a complex language; a sermon of combustion and fusion, booming like the voice of God.

The sliding door behind me opens with a sharp clap. I am awakened to the enormity of what I have been feeling, but in the moment of realization the feeling is gone—vaporous morning dew rising off garden moss. The tatami remain cool to the touch. The maples in the garden are still verdant, swaying back and forth in the gentle breeze like kelp in ocean waves. The uguisu is gone without trace. An elderly couple who just entered the room sit quietly in the corner opposite me. Did they notice that I was on fire, burning in unison with the universe? Did they see the warbler flitting through my branches, chirping in my ear?

In some way it remains with me, the unity, the instant of being whole, not separated into nature or man but simply alive. Complete in the moment. Still tingling, I feel anew the indivisibility of nature; that we cannot separate ourselves from the rest of the natural world by any of our acts. Rather we come to see that those acts are simply *our nature*. We do them because we are capable of them; they are inherent in us. We kill and ruin not because we are unnatural but because it is within our nature to do so. Likewise, we cannot elevate ourselves above nature on any testimonial to the refinement of our character. We design and create not because we are supranatural, but simply because those qualities also are in our nature. We do all these things as naturally as the uguisu flies and sings.

It is in our nature to build and to create, as much as it is to be wild and brute. When the wild calls, I will run through the mountains and sweat, give blood to leeches that cling to grasses by clear streams. But when struck by the muse to create, I will make a garden, be an artist in nature, for gardens reveal to us what is best in our nature. The garden is a place for the gentle builder and humble artist to call their home, a place for them, and all those who visit thereafter, to find their way back to a unified world where there are no boundaries. No point where the garden ends and the mountain begins.

CLOSING THE CIRCLE

THIS COUNTRY HOUSE IS OLD. THE WOOD OF THE OPEN CORRIDOR that runs along the outside is weathered deeply, its grain as pronounced as the lines raked in the sand of the garden. On the edge of the corridor, just by the base of one of the posts that holds up the eaves, is an emerald green grasshopper, brilliant against the deep umber of the wood. I watch it and wonder if it, too, has a locust within? It twitches, flexes its wings, lies still for a while, then jumps and clatters into the garden.

The garden is a simple rectangle of coarse, white sand, now mellowed by the afternoon sun. Unlike the borderless pond garden I wrote of before that dissolved seamlessly into the forest, this garden is entirely enclosed. On three sides are wooden buildings and on the fourth, the side opposite of where I sit, is a low wall of charred wooden boards. The sand is luminous, the wall matte-black, like the scrim hung at the rear of a stage to lend it depth. Just chest high, it abuts one of the buildings that enclose the garden on the left side, but to the right, it disappears into a jumble of vines that have worked their way up and over from outside. One delicate young shoot probes far out across the face of the wall, tracing a zigzag path, heart-shaped leaves extending left, then right, then left again: light green stepping stones crossing a scorched field.

Outside the wall, the land drops off steeply into a deep valley, rising again far off in a series of ever higher mountain ranges, but from the veranda where I sit, the wall conceals the middle ground—the valley and lower hills—leaving only garden, wall, and mountains in view, layered against one another like a misty Sung ink landscape. Unlike the mountain where the uguisu lives, which embraces temple and pond and gentles them in its shadow, the landscape here expands in sweeping gestures of light and space. Only the wall gives form to the garden.

Raked into the sand is a circle, small ridges making patterns of white on white, which in this waxing light are tinted russet on one side and light blue on the other, the hues of shadows on snowdrifts. The lines in the sand radiate outward, like ripples from a pebble thrown into a still pond, yet these go nowhere. Enjoying the mildly hallucinatory effect of watching them, I recall another circle, drawn just this morning in my studio far back down the mountain, in the center of Kyoto.

The sun had risen over the hills that border the city not long before, and a strong, clear light filled the room, palpably, like scented air. On one high, white wall I hung a large sheet of paper, set the point of a long bar-compass in the center, and drew a circle, slowly, carefully, watching the silver pen-tip as it moved across the blank page. Concentrating on the pale-blue line flowing from the pen, I became detached from the action, as if just lying back on a grassy riverbank, watching contrail from a jet circling very high up in a cloudless sky, but with the colors in reverse.

As the line drew out, a story revealed itself; one that I now understand led me here, to this garden. It began at the top of the page, where the line, newly drawn and glistening wet, was no more than a dash—a mark enticing to the curiosity but without immediate or tangible meaning. As the line lengthened, however, drawing out across the page, it formed a small crescent, like a bent bow or the curve of a satellite dish. Line becoming object. Arcing down to the bottom of the page, then rising again in a pendulum curve back toward the top, the line changed in quality again. Unlike the crescent (a thing more opened than closed) it began to define the edge of an object, an area becoming enfolded by slow degrees. What had seemed so wide-open was becoming partially shut, the uniform field of white beginning to have within it a separate space that had not been there before, divided ephemerally yet unmistakably from its surroundings, like that part of the ocean encircled by a fisherman's net. Line becoming object becoming space.

When there was no more than two hand-widths of the line left to be drawn, I had a strange experience, an optical illusion I think, though it may have been real. I began to see the as-yet-undrawn line: an illusory line existing exactly where the blue line would be when I completed the circle. The apparition was not clear, or a shadow; it was more like the air had simply thickened along that route and was bending light. If I had tried, I could have completed the circle freehand, just following the path prescribed by the ghostly image.

I think this is the nature of things, if not always, at least at times; they exist even before they have form—are simply waiting to be filled in like the empty spaces in a coloring book. A song exists, unwritten, unsung, hovering nearby a musician's ear who suddenly finds herself composing with inexplicable fluidity; an athlete sees himself crossing a high-jump bar, feels his back curve, the weight of his head falling, a muscular jerk as his feet flip upward at exactly the right moment. He senses all this first, and then he jumps, simply filling in the image with the reality of his body, as if sliding through an opening in the air.

As the line neared completion, I was filled with the expectancy of a child who, having shuffled himself full of static on a carpet, nears his finger to a metal doorknob incrementally and awaits the spark. When the line finally closed—one finely etched, shimmering, damp blue line overlapping a dull, dry one—and as the space inside the circle became entire and complete, I heard a faint click and hum, like an electric current being switched on.

I read about a painting contest won by drawing a circle. The story was that all the contestants who had gathered for the day were given a set amount of time in which to produce their work, but even after the judges gave the signal to begin, one of them just sat before his easel looking at the empty canvas. As the allotted time was coming to a close, he reached out, took up his brush, and drew a perfect circle . . . freehand. Was it the perfection of the form or the simplicity of the design, or maybe just the boldness of the idea that made the judges award him the day? Perhaps it was some potency inherent in circles that sparked their interest, as it has for Zen priests who paint circles called *enso* as symbols of enlightenment, the universal potential of the human mind. In *mandala*, the circle represents wisdom, which together with reason, symbolized by the lotus blossom, are the dual aspects of Buddha. Wisdom and reason: what nobler ambitions have we?

I had a reason for drawing that circle this morning. Not one so lofty as wisdom or enlightenment. I was trying to model the skin of the Earth, the layer of air and water that wraps our planet and constitutes the boundaries of the space we live within. I wanted to get a grasp on the scale of that fluid sheathing, to try to understand it from a new perspective, not from within the way we all do during our daily lives, but from outside, looking down on it objectively the way only astronauts can. I decided the best way to start was to take a look at the whole thing in cross-section.

First I looked up the heights of the lowest and highest points on Earth, starting with the deepest part of the ocean, the bottom of the Mariana Trench off Guam in the Pacific Ocean, and then up to the crest of Mount Everest—in all about a 20,000-meter spread. Of course the atmosphere goes up higher, much higher than Everest, but I was interested only in our realm of experience, so I approximated and stuck to the limits of the folded planet crust. Next, I chose a drafting pen from among my tools and filled it with pale-blue ink, drew a clean line on a page, and measured it to be about one and a half millimeters thick. Calculated against the average diameter of the earth, I figured I would need to draw a circle about a meter in diameter in order to get it all to scale. So that's what I did—drew a meter-wide circle in light-blue ink, just over a millimeter thick, on a stark white sheet of paper taped to the wall of my studio.

I drew the circle—the atmosphere and oceans to scale—then stood back on the other side of the room and looked at what I had done. Took a good, long look at our Earth in cross-section and just stood there, dumfounded, struck still, like a tornado survivor who emerges from the safety of his cellar to a shattered world, blinking at the unrecognizable. A line drawn to scale, representing all depth and height that this planet has to offer and from twenty feet, it could hardly be seen. Worse yet, I realized the drawing was an exaggeration; it was too *thick*. Nothing lives on the top of Everest, forgetting bacteria, and hardly anything, other than microbes perhaps, lives down in the Mariana Trench.

In fact, virtually all life on this planet exists in a narrow band, perhaps only 4,000 meters thick, extending between the upper layers of the ocean to which sufficient sunlight penetrates and the point in the atmosphere where the oxygen gets too thin, about 3,500 meters above sea level. As I stood squinting at that fine blue line from across the room, I tried to envision another line that would represent the reality of life on Earth—an even thinner line, just a hair's breadth, embedded inside the first. I imagined it to be light green, or at least I tried to, standing there peering intently from across the room, hoping to will into the fragile blue line a place I could believe in, no matter how ephemeral, something that would give even the slightest semblance of home—a scent, a whisper, a touch. Yet none came.

The phone rang but I didn't answer it. I couldn't. It rang itself out. I swung open the window to get some air, breathing slow, chest tight. Outside, on the street far below, cars ran silently, oblivious. A bus pulled over, spilling uniformed schoolgirls into the street, laughing, teasing, bunched together affectionately, completely unaware of the frailty of the world they bubbled through so giddily. The city spread out beyond them, stretching eastward over to a range of low mountains: tiled roofs of old townhouses just below, cascading like silver-black waves along the narrow streets; a young couple standing in front of the shadowed entrance to a love hotel, hesitant, nervous, intent; the Kamo River, flowing quietly, it too tracing a shimmering blue line. So much detail, so many things, so many nooks and crannies: powerlines in snags over the streets; business signs hawking from the corners of every building; a pagoda like a Chinese puzzle in the distance; on the slope of the hill, a graveyard, from here looking like a large parking lot; nearby the graves a towering, serene statue of Kannon, the *bodhisattva* of compassion; and behind it all, the mountains, a wall of lush green trees. "How many leaves on a tree," I wondered, "How many trees on the mountain; how many mountains in Japan; in the world?" The numbers rise in exponential surges—the mind strives to follow, fails, and freezes.

I glanced back across the room to the drawing on the wall. A tiny insect with ultrafine lace wings flew in the window and landed on the illuminated blue screen of my computer, translucent. I looked at it, and back at the circle, but it just made no sense. Where in the thin blue line, where in that finer green line that I couldn't imagine let alone draw, was all of this? The lace-winged fly, the computer, the city, the countless leaves on countless trees? Walking the earth, right down here, close in where you can feel the street, smell the soil, the world seems so riddled with complexities, so subtle, so immense, and there I found myself faced with the reality that the whole thing is no more than lichen on rock.

❀   ❀   ❀

That was this morning. After that I ran. Leaving the drawing, I hurried out as fast as I could, cycled home, got in the car and left for the countryside. The road out of Kyoto to the west rose quickly into the forested mountains that enclose the city. The mountains are not high but they are steep, and the road soon dwindled to a three-meter lane, too narrow for two cars to pass, switching back and forth in hairpins along the slopes of narrow valleys. It had been built for foot-travel, not cars, and the tires slipped and squealed at each turn. Far below, in the depths of the slender valley, narrow strips of flat bottom land had been turned into rice paddies; the slopes above them held small orchards of citrus trees, their sweet blossoms scenting the air. Yet, soon the mountain became too steep for even orchards and all that remained were dense plantations of slender cryptomeria trees and untended forests of scrub oaks and maples. Beneath the fine branching of the forest canopy, a sea of chest-high grass bamboo extended in all directions. Sunlight shot flickering through the leaves of the forest, dappling across the broad bamboo leaves. A river far below crashed white over massive boulders on its way down to Kyoto; the indigo sky fell in patches through the cover of trees, fleetingly. I slowed the car and rolled the window all the way down, wondering what it would be like to be in this forest, as part of it, not as a traveler gliding through untouched?

Throw a seed into the forest and it must fight to survive, but if by chance it lands in a place where it touches the ground and gets a little light, it will grow. If a wildcat from the zoo were released into that wood, it too could survive. With its thick fur, claws, and acute sense of smell, it could fend for itself. Freed from its cage, it may even relish the experience. But were I to try the same thing—release myself into the forest—I fear it would not go so well.

I began to imagine the possibility: stopping the car, turning off the engine and walking away, key in place. Stripping down buck-naked, leaving behind all trace of civilization, striding off into the ocean of dappled bamboo leaves. After an initial thrill of gentle sunlight on bare skin, the whole experience would undoubtedly turn sour: bamboo leaves cutting fine slashes through my unprotected skin, rocks tearing at the skin of my feet, no food, no shelter. In the wild without cover or community, I might last a week or two, it's spring after all, but no more. If it were winter, though, the landscape would swallow me whole in a day and I would dissolve into it like a fallen leaf. As beautiful and enticing as the wild is, I am not of it entirely.

I drove on for another half hour, thoughts of being consumed by the wild forest lingering like the echo of a song repeating in the mind of its own accord, and then the forest opened up, becoming lighter as it gave way to rice fields and then to a small farming hamlet. The fields had just been planted—much earlier here than in town because it is colder and the rice will take that much longer to grow—and the rows of fine green rice shoots appeared to hover in blue sky reflecting in the dark paddy water. The paddies descended the slope in terraced layers, each a blue oval patch, pieces of the sky torn off and scattered on the ground.

On the other side of the hamlet, where the road began to drop back down into a valley, was the house I'm in now, and as I approached I realized what had driven me to come out this way. The garden. Parking on the side of the road in front of the house, I walked halfway up the front path, but seeing that nobody was in, stopped and went around the back way, through a bamboo grove and up the hill to the rear of the house. Letting myself in the back gate, I walked over to the garden and found that it was covered with tufts of moss that had rolled down off the steep thatched roof. I set about cleaning: sweeping, picking out stubborn pieces, nicking a weed or two. Cleaning is calming, and the shock of my morning discovery, and the ghosts of the wild forest, felt more distant as the garden cleared of debris.

There is a spiral of moss beneath an old maple tree, but

other than that the garden is simply a broad sheet of white sand. Having cleared the sand of debris and weeds, I flattened it with a toothless rake built for the purpose. The sand became peaceful, dampened, like a ringing bell touched lightly by a finger. Next, using a toothed rake, the weight of which felt good, I raked into the sand long straight lines that ran the entire length of the garden, giving the surface the texture of coarse corduroy. And then, at last, I did what I always do when I come to this place. On top of those lines, I raked a circle in the sand, walking backwards so as to erase my own footsteps. The rake had eight teeth, and as I pulled, eight fine lines, eight parallel valleys, traced into the coarse sand. As with the circle in my studio, the lines developed from an initial impression in the sand into a crescent and finally, coming full circle, the teeth of the rake docked neatly with the beginnings of the valleys and the space within the circle snapped into focus, suddenly becoming an entity that it had not been until that moment. This time, there was no electric sound, no click and hum, but the effect of closing the circle, of creating a space within space, was just as powerful.

Henry Moore, the English sculptor, related a experience that he had while carving a plaster model. He was digging a hollow with his knife further and further into the white mass, deepening the shadow, when he unexpectedly broke through to the other side and the pocket he was carving out suddenly became a hole letting light flash in from the other side. I imagine he felt as if he were peeking into a new, as yet unexplored, world. In the completed sculpture, much larger and made of cast bronze, there is a hole, but not the epiphany he experienced while making it, of breaking through the very last thin layer into enlightenment. The result of the creative process is presented to the viewer but not the moment of creation itself. There is something, then, in the artistic experience, in the moment of creation, that is entirely unto itself, private, and untransferable. That's why I like raking sand so much. An infinitely reusable canvas, it offers unlimited moments of creation.

But there was something more to drawing the circle in the sand than feeling the moment of creation—it was about defining the edge, creating an enclosure, a symbolic reflection of the wall that encloses the garden. If I was looking for boundaries and finding none in the temple with the pond garden, if there the edges there were all blurred into a mountain forest, here I was making boundaries; defining a place to make it *be*.

The English word "garden" means enclosure, or at least it used to, stemming from more ancient words, such as the Germanic *gardaz*, which meant to grasp or enclose. A garden in its original form was simply a safe haven, a plot of land enclosed, bordered off from the great wilderness. The *gardaz* was the enclosing wall—not the space held within. The fundamental act of gardening, therefore, is not the collection of plants, or the use of water, or the decoration of the outdoor environment, but simply the act of creating a space, enclosed and separate from the wild: a niche to feel safe inside of. The garden is the circle.

In Japan there are ceremonial gatherings, called *chakai*, where guests are invited to drink whisked green tea in small rustic teahouses. Each teahouse has a garden, called a *chaniwa* or *roji*, that acts as an entryway. The gathering is intended to heighten the awareness of the participants, physically, aesthetically, and spiritually. The tea garden acts as a stage for inward preparation before the event. When the guests arrive (usually no more than four or five people) they enter the garden through an outer gate that delineates the threshold between the inner world of the tea gathering and the profane world outside, filing in quietly in order, the most proficient, eldest, or honored guest going first, and the second in rank among them coming up last.

There are certain responsibilities associated with being last in line, the first of which is to close the outer gate. Having entered, the final guest gently closes the doors and slides a long wooden bar across them to bolt them shut and close off the outer world. The creak of the hinges and dull sound of wood tapping wood carries forward through the garden, alerting the host of his guests' arrival. For the guests the sound carries a more potent meaning—once heard, they are no longer of the ordinary world.

In Europe, the ancients piled rocks in lines, or pounded rows of rough stakes into the ground and wove them with coarse vine wattle, to make their *gardaz*, separating themselves from the wild just enough feel safe. Medieval Japanese teamasters designed a more elegant threshold—refined fences of bamboo or clay-plastered walls—but their intent was not all that different: to create an enclosure and by that separate the inner world from the outer. No matter the material, no matter the aesthetic, the act of making the enclosure—of closing the circle—marks the beginning of the garden.

I realize now, in looking on the garden before me and reflecting on the day, that the initial creation of the *gardaz* stemmed from exactly the fear of being consumed by the wild that I so recklessly toyed with—from our primeval ancestors staring into the shadows of the forest and praying for the solace of a tempered world. Gardens were later built within those enclosures to elicit the wild by recomposing its elements in such a way that better suited the needs of the gardener. In a world too vast to comprehend, too powerful to come to terms with, the garden was a way to adjust the wild to the scale of human measurement. First enclosure, then garden, and last, as the story comes full circle, a garden without boundaries in which the enclosing wall disappears, the edges blur, and only a subtle tempering of the garden distinguishes it from its surroundings.

58

Yet the circle drawn in my studio this morning did not suggest a limitless world, too vast and powerful to comprehend, but an ephemeral one, clinging to the surface of the globe with no more tenacity than the moss on these garden stones. Where then in the garden is solace for the mind that has looked back on the world from beyond the limits of the atmosphere and found nothing but frailty and insignificance?

The grasshopper pops out from under the veranda, bounding halfway across the garden into the circle of sand. It waits, resting, but the shadow of the wall has stretched across the garden and it doesn't linger long in the cool air. With a click and a whir it jumps again, landing on the silver-tile top of the wall, then once more, into the valley and gone. The blackened wall separates the garden from the mountains beyond, and yet it also connects the two, drawing the distant view of nature forward into the artistic composition of the garden.

Contradictory as this may seem, the act of separation is also a means of association. Like the backyard gardens of Korean country estates that simply wall in a section of a grassy mountain and do no more, the wall brings a section of the wild into the sphere of a human order and in doing so also allows those who reside within, in reverse, a means to approach the wild. The enclosure transcends its role as separator, becoming a coupling instead.

In closing the circle—closing the gate, building the wall—we shut out the wild with the intent of protecting ourselves but in doing so we also create a place in which we can be at one with our environment: a garden. At home in the garden, we find that through the garden we are joined to the larger natural world. The garden becomes a stepping stone, a bridge beyond social boundaries back to the wild. Within the enclosure of the garden we feel safe from the terrors of that wilderness and, at the same time, at one with it, accepting of both its power and fragility, for we recognize in it ourselves. Our limits no longer defined by our skin, we become the moss, the sand, and the wall, the finely traced vine; the distant mountains with countless leaves on countless trees.

59

TREES

I WOKE THIS MORNING TO THE DRY SOUND OF WIND RUSTLING through bamboo in the garden; a tiny bell hung beneath the eaves was tinkling quietly. I got up and got out, urged eastward by the breeze and a memory, following them to the backstreets that trace the base of the mountains, twisting with each fold in the landscape. The sounds and scents of the city—a dull whine of traffic, fish grilling—grew fainter as I walked, and the clamor of the avenues turned quietly into an old neighborhood. High above, summer clouds moved in a slow procession east toward the hills and over to Lake Biwa, gliding smoothly as if on plate glass, their shadows chasing after them across the landscape.

Following the clouds, I neared the foothills where the streets narrow sharply, bordered on both sides by stone walls. Although the walls are low, at most no higher than my knee, each is topped by a neatly clipped hedge, a wooden fence, or an occasional earthen wall softened by time, completing an enclosure of green and sepia that shelters the lanes, making them worlds unto themselves. Behind the walls and hedges are garden trees and tiled roofs of old wooden houses, and behind them, occasionally, a glimpse to the nearby mountains where the leaves flicker green and white, nuzzled by passing breezes. The sun was warm and the sheltered lane a pleasant place to be. Something in the air and light reminded me of the first time I came to that lane and discovered what I have come back to find today.

There was a warm breeze that day too, nudging and guiding, suggesting left or right with subtle gusts. There was a breeze and there was a cat, thin and black, that appeared suddenly from below a wooden fence, pushing its way out through a row of dense azaleas. It froze, sniffed the air, then prowled down the alley in front of me, a jet-black splash following tightly along the base of brown walls, shadow within shadow, lithe and furtive. It seemed to lead; I seemed to follow, and we walked that way for some time before parting in front of an old wooden gate overhung by a large pine tree. I lingered to look—and the cat was gone.

The gate was inset in a long earthen wall, about as tall as I am, which had weathered and been repaired so many times it had become a mosaic, barklike, a quilt of clay and time. Trees from the garden hung over the wall in places, neatly pruned yet grown beyond containment: the pine by the gate and further down along the wall a maple, a cherry, and a large osmanthus, the petalless orange flowers of which would scent the air in autumn. The cherry was old and leaned out over the lane. Its gnarled black trunk was bent in such a way that it cut through the wall, or rather, the wall had been constructed so as to avoid the trunk, gracefully circumventing it, allowing room in which the cherry could grow. The curved gap between wall and tree, half filled with dappled shadows, seemed to hold a message, like an oracle bone glinting from deep within a cave.

I ran my hand along the bark of the cherry, patting it to feel its density; touched lightly the opening in the clay wall where it skirted the tree. There was language in the very shape of its curve, in the separation yet unity of tree and wall, an intention given form, expressive though silent. The owner of the garden had a choice: cut the tree, or notch the wall. It would have been easier for the builder to remove the tree, yet they chose instead to defer to it—because of its age, because of the generous blossoms with which it painted the lane each spring, because it gave them a pleasure that outweighed the convenience of construction. Be-

65

cause in some way, however small, to them the tree was sacred.

There are many sacred trees in Japan. Some are to be found in forests, others within shrine precincts; all are envisioned as links between the world of the gods and the earthly realm. Most shrines have a cluster of such trees that are allowed to grow wild, or almost wild. In larger shrines, those clusters can amount to small forests while in lesser shrines they may be relegated to only a handful of lanky trees and shrubs, squeezed into the narrow space between shrine building and the surrounding wall, taking up precious space but always, *always*, allowed their presence, as if the shrines could not exist without them. And so they couldn't.

In the south of Kyoto, in a place altogether unlike this quiet lane, is a shrine with an immense sacred tree. The road there is wide, rumbling with heavy traffic that settles a gritty dust on everything. Thirty years ago the neighborhood around the shrine experienced a small economic boom; the city government nodded in its direction just long enough to install a metal arcade along the street to shade the front of the shops, hanging it with orange plastic lights, like sad white flowers blossoming from within split pumpkins. But the city's interest was passing, and time has not been kind. The arcade is streaked with rust and sags in places, the stores are less busy than they used to be, and the neighborhood now embodies the hardness and desolation particular to cities.

The shrine faces the road, separated from it by a low fence of chiseled granite. A short flight of stone stairs leads up from the sidewalk to the shrine grounds, at the top of which, just to the left, is the tree, girdled with the thick straw rope that marks it as sacred. A camphor, its glossy leaves give off an aromatic, mothball scent when crushed. When I first saw the tree some years ago, I had been cycling, lost in thought, eyes to the pavement. Rounding an easy bend, I looked up by chance and stopped still at the sight. Within the context of its environs, the camphor was simply unbelievable, alien yet resplendent. Impossibly large, it towered over shrine and street, shading generously in all directions. It is the kind of tree that humbles those who come before it, making them feel small within the world. Yet it was not just its size that set it apart from what surrounded it; there was also some quality inherent to the tree that was lacking elsewhere. A monument of wild nature, it had become engulfed within a tide of shabby, box-like buildings and stood among them sublime in its incongruity, mooring the neighborhood to its past, to an ancient, long-forgotten forest soul.

Just inside the entrance to the shrine, sheltered beneath a low roof, was a stone trough overflowing with clear spring water that flowed into it from the mouth of a bronze dragon. Wooden ladles were arranged on the edge of the trough for visitors to use. I took a cupful to rinse my mouth, another for my hands, a last cupful for the cup, cleansing the vessel of cleansing. Ladle laid to rest, I went to the tree, to where the braided roots buckled upward around the base of the trunk.

The bark was deeply grooved in patches, and from the rope tied around its girth hung two strips of white paper folded into zigzags like lightning. Two lines of ants marched on the trunk: one going up, the other down. The ants nest amid the roots of the tree; their food is in the leafy crown, and so each day they march up and down the bark the way sap flows inside. The up-line made a detour around the empty nymphal case of a cicada larvae that still clung to the bark with its sharp claws, a dry ghost. I plucked it off and looked closely at the perfect mask, a detailed, hollow casting. The back of the shell was split open; the cicada had metamorphosed and gone. What crawled out of the soil and this far up the trunk had completed its journey to the top of the tree on a clatter of wings.

Cicadas swarmed in the crown of the tree, emitting a slow whirring that rose and fell in cycles. Inadvertently, birds that had come to hunt them brought other life; a tuft of grass seeded in that way grew out from the crotch of a branch. Just above it, a movement in a limb-hollow hinted at a hidden nest. I thought at first it might be a *musasabi*, a flying squirrel, but saw it was just a bird's nest. In the evening, I imagined crows would gather in the tree on their way to the hills. They'd caw and circle, descending on the crown like pilgrims to the shrine, filling its branches with black noise. Such a tree is more than just a tree; it is a community, an ecosystem unto itself. Of course, dependent on the tree are the ants and cicadas and boisterous crows, but the associations are far more complex, amplifying where the tree attenuates—in its leaves and roots.

Despite the thinness of a leaf, packed within it are thousands of chloroplasts, waferlike platelets of chlorophyll. The chloroplasts absorb sunlight, using that electromagnetic energy to create chemical energy, transforming water and carbon dioxide into oxygen and carbohydrates. The oxygen is released while the carbohydrates remain within the plant as energy for its growth.

The system is fascinating for several reasons, the first having to do with the surprisingly important role of chlorophyll in the larger scheme of things.

Although we can extract energy from many sources—tidal,

geothermal, nuclear—the source we make the most regular use of is the sun. Some solar energy is derived from wind and ocean currents (which are initiated by solar heat), but most of it comes from plants. The energy we derive from our food, for instance, whether vegetable or animal, began initially as sunlight captured by chlorophyll in plants. Likewise, the energy provided by the fuels we use, whether logs, coal, oil, or gas, was initially electromagnetic energy converted to chemical energy within a leaf. Leaves are where sunlight is forged into a usable form, a process without which it would be just so many photons bouncing around the planet, brilliant but unusable, and Earth no more than a hot rock. Individually microscopic, yet global in extent, chlorophyll molecules mark the boundary where electromagnetic radiation from the sun synergizes with organic life.

69

Another fascinating thing about chlorophyll is that it appears to *not* be inherent to plants; originally it existed as a separate entity and was incorporated into primordial botanical life in a symbiotic relationship, like algae and fungus in lichen. Like mitochondria, chloroplasts have their own DNA encoding that is separate from that of their host's. Whereas the "greenness" of a leaf seems an essential part of a tree, it is in fact a guest within a community.

❀   ❀   ❀

The ants returning from the crown of the tree each carry a morsel in their mandibles gleaned from the higher reaches. They swirl down and around, descending into their hole. Underground, they burrow among the camphor's complex root system, tunneling through vast underground networks of soil fungi called mycelium. At points the mycelium fuses with root hairs to form mycorrhizae, "tree-roots," which are mutually beneficial to both tree and fungi. Through its connection to the widespread fungal network, the tree gets a vastly increased root surface area to absorb water and nutrients; in return, the fungi get energy-rich sugars and amino acids from the tree that they (having no chlorophyll) cannot produce themselves.

An experiment with soil fungi was run recently employing piles of oil-soaked soil. Some were inoculated with fungi spores; the rest were treated in various other ways. All were covered with sheets and allowed to incubate. To the surprise of the researchers, when the sheets were removed those piles inoculated with spores were sprouting mushrooms and the soil was free of oil; nor, tests later showed, did the fungus contain polycarbons. The fungal growth didn't absorb the oil, it consumed it, carbon chain by carbon chain.

I imagine the camphor tree's roots stretching wide beneath it, linked in turn to a massive fungal net permeating the soil beneath the shrine, beneath the sidewalk and the road, beneath the city. Whatever percolates into the soil from urban deposits—asphalt and tar laid on the road, oil and gasoline dripped from countless cars, effluent from local businesses—is consumed by the fungi, and at the center of it, towering over it all, the camphor, feeding the web that cleanses the earth. At one end of this scheme, the sun, a fusion explosion pumping out electromagnetic energy; at the other, the earth, a mute mineral globe. Between the two rise the trees, leaves rich with chlorophyll, roots deep in fungi, and through their complex community (part biotic, part chemical), sun and earth fuse.

The people in ancient times, who first girdled the trunk of the camphor with a thick rope and made prayers before the tree, knew nothing of chloroplasts and mycorrhizae. The microscopic intricacies of the extensive biochemical ecosystem, of which the tree itself is only a small part, were unknown to them, and yet they had an intrinsic understanding of trees as life-giving and as being integral with larger worlds—natural and sacred—an understanding that led them to call trees like the camphor in the shrine *yorishiro*, Vessels of the God Spirit. Amorphous, complex, and mysterious, the Spirit was seen as permeating all nature, flowing through all things, binding them in a unity. We analyze and quantify—count chlorophyll bundles, measure inconceivable miles of fungal strands—yet the tree remains a mystery. It transforms sunlight and we build our world . . . it harbors the God Spirit and we nurture our souls.

❋   ❋   ❋

I left the shrine with the intent of circling the block to try and see the camphor from other angles but found instead another tree, a strangely formed plane tree, its white and gray-green bark mottled in a patchwork like the old clay wall. It had been planted too close to the street and, as it grew, its bark began to touch the tubular steel guardrails that separate sidewalk from street. Over the years the bark had swelled and enveloped the tubes, enfolding them inside the tree itself, so at that one point, iron fence and tree fused—metallurgy and botany, civilization and nature, melded there into a single thought.

Left to their own devices, in a hundred years or so, all the plane trees along the street might eventually do the same thing;

so that in time, segments along the entire metal barricade would be consumed . . . then the street . . . then the city. Seeds would settle in cracks, roothairs pierce the smallest fissures and expand, shoots swell and flush, until everything was blanketed by trees, like the halls of Angkor Wat, asphalt shattered and returning to soil, weathered concrete cool and mossy beneath a huge extended forest canopy—the wild rebounding.

Turning a corner, I headed down a narrow alley that led behind the shrine. Higher buildings by the street gave way to lower wooden residences, all built in the postwar push to develop the area. Each house had a concrete-block wall along its front, weathered and pitted, some leaning, all streaked darkly by black rain. A small brook that used to flow through the area now trickled along in a deep concrete culvert on the side of the alley; some cigarette packets and magazines lay sodden, plastered to the bottom. Until just thirty years ago, all this land was rice fields and meadows; the shrine stood in that open landscape among them. And there among the hardened fields, I found yet another tree, an old hemlock that also had a rope wrapped around it to mark it as sacred, though the rope was very thin and simply made. The hemlock grew out of an implausibly small triangle of land, a remnant patch of soil squeezed between a culvert, concrete wall, and rusty fence, tilting out over the alley, looking surprisingly healthy for the conditions it grew under.

Closing my eyes I saw the city expand from its medieval core at the center of the valley, spread outward like a surge tide rising over a beachhead that it submerges until none but the tips of lonely rocks show through. The city covered the meadow that once quilted the slope in greens and browns; erased small thickets and groves of low trees that bordered the meadows; sucked rambling brooks down into concrete culverts; covered over rice paddies one by one as their owners sold off their land to feed the city's hunger. The expansion nudged in toward the hemlock, getting closer by degrees, consuming every last scrap of land, until it reached to the very roots of the tree . . . and then it stopped.

Across the city, scattered here and there within the carpet of buildings, patches of green still showed through the development, each one an ancient tree, a *yorishiro*, towering above the shops and houses surrounding it like rocks above the tide. If you were to walk through the city and seek them out, you would find beneath each tree a shrine. I opened my eyes and the hemlock shone out, sparkling like after a summer shower.

Cities expand. Why not? . . . so does the universe. It is thought, however, that if the average density of matter in the universe is high enough, it will also eventually collapse—Big Bang to Big Crunch. The theory used to be that the universe will, in time, fall in upon itself, becoming increasingly, and inconceivably, small, dense, and hot, collapsing down to the size of a galaxy, of a planet, a grain of sand, and so on, to infinity . . . until there is nothing. Then came the development of String theory, a branch of physics that sheds light on the elusive link between special relativity (the world of the very small) and general relativity (that of the very big).

According to the mathematics of String theory, as things shrink to very small sizes, very strange things happen. As lengths dwindle lower than the Planck length, just a millionth of a billionth of a billionth of a billionth of a centimeter, the mathematics of things getting smaller becomes identical to that of things getting larger. The universe does not, according to String theory, shrink to a point infinitely small but only to the Planck length from which it rebounds, and reexpands . . . a cosmic heartbeat.

We push back the wild to build our cities, elbowing aside things sacred in search of convenience. We push and push and push until it seems that we'll scrape the planet clean and yet, even in Kyoto, a city in one of the planet's most densely populated countries, sacred trees remain. Caught between concrete walls, crowded in by construction, growing in but the barest patches of soil . . . yet they remain. This is not the vengeance of nature, like plane trees consuming the city whole, nor is it a protective aura, a magic spell that prevents sacred trees from being felled (at times they are). What saves them is not within them at all; it is within *us*. We shunt and cast aside nature like a universe collapsing, and cast ourselves down with it until we reach a certain point, a kind of Planck length of the soul, beyond which we can go no further, and there we stop. We bear down on the shrine with its majestic camphor, cut and clear the forest that once surrounded it; we build right up to the roots of the hemlock, reduce it to a lonely anachronism by a hard road, but, in the end, we leave those trees. We must. They are sacred to us. We collapse in against ourselves to the point where we meet our limit—at the hemlock by the brook-in-culvert, at the camphor filled with whirring cicadas— and there we pause, and from that most intensely compressed point, we rebound and find our sacred world again.

❀ ❀ ❀

There is another sacred tree I know well, a cedar tree deep in the woods at the top of a mountain in northern Kyoto. The thing about it that takes me back each year to visit is that it is dead.

The mountain itself is sacred, interspersed from top to bottom with shrines and temples of various sizes, some new, others as old as the forest itself. At several points along the climb to the summit, ancient cedar trees border the path, hung with thick straw ropes. They guard the sanctity of the mountain, yet more than that religious symbolism, what impresses me most each time I see them is simply their primal vitality. The obvious physical strength of the trees itself is reassuring; the massive woody columns seem an embodiment of the force of life itself.

In contrast to those vital trees, at the top of the mountain, just by the side of the path, is the stump of a cedar that fell in a typhoon some years ago. What remains of the tree is still taller than I, but the bark has lost its hue and has begun to moss over in places. Despite the fact that it is no longer living, it still is honored with a straw rope—renewed each year—and in front of it stands a small shrine at which offerings of sake, salt, and rice are made. The tree did not lose its distinction as sacred because it died; it is still honored and will be until what remains has completely rotted away and dissolved back into the earth.

In fact, it will continue to be honored beyond even then. Just at the foot of the tree a cedar seedling pokes out from the roots of the old tree, nourishing itself on the fallen tree. Most likely the sapling was planted by one of the priests who care for the mountain, a way to link old to new. The idea of honoring a life beyond life is not uncommon for people to apply to people whom they have loved or respected. What brings me back to this tree is that I am astonished, and pleased, that the same reverence would be extended to a tree.

✽   ✽   ✽

In the quiet lane, amid the sheltering hedges and fences, I come again to the cherry pushing through the earth wall. It casts a long shadow across the pitted clay surface onto the street. Finding a spot to sit just across the lane from the tree, I begin to sketch: a fern poking out from the stone foundation of the wall, the rhythmic play of light and shadow on the tiles that form its cap, a shoot with three green leaves sprouting from the side of the gnarled trunk, new life sprung from old. I record each detail as faithfully as possible, imprinting them as much in my thoughts as with graphite on paper, yet as I begin to draw the crown of the tree, I find myself simplifying; capturing each leaf is a task I'm not up to.

Drawing, I remember a meeting with architects who were designing a large structure in Osaka; a computer-generated video image of the proposed building was being screened for the owner. The room was dark; a deep, pulsating techno-thrum reverberated seductively from the monitor. The camera appeared to zoom in on the building, floated weightlessly into and through the structure, sheets of glass exuding light, lingering on the details of the architecture: the grillwork on each step of the escalators; a glittering mid-air sculpture; anodized steel rods stabilizing a curtain wall, each flange depicted perfectly. The camera backed out through the glass into the courtyard to admire the exterior again . . . and then it happened. The trees in the courtyard came into view, but unlike the architecture, which was portrayed with precise photorealism, the trees looked like paper cutouts, each leaf a simple quadrangle, as if they were made of confetti sprinkled on a sticky wire frame. Whereas the computer could generate an image of a multistory architectural structure in excellent and subtle detail, and sail through it effortlessly, were it to try to portray that level of detail on a single tree (let alone a courtyard-full) the calculations would freeze the CPU. Trees are simply that complex.

The black cat has come back to the alley and rolls about playfully. It sniffs at the air, circles a few times, then jumps, slipping gracefully through the gap between cherry and wall, a shadow returning to its source, through the hole and gone. I finish my sketch and go over to the wall, peek through the gap to see where it went. Although I cannot see the whole garden, what I can see appears like a scroll painting: a waterfall spills out of the darkness of trees, a stream meanders and disappears behind large bushes at the foot of a large black pine, stones along its banks punctuate and modulate the flow. The plants in the garden are mainly evergreen: pine, azalea, camellia, and osmanthus. The overall form of the garden—created by stones, soil, and those evergreen plants—remains basically unchanged throughout the year. The plants that do mark the change of the seasons with color or scent do so in measured quantities, and when they pass, the body of the garden still remains.

But this was not always so; a thousand years ago, perennial flowers and grasses—the ephemeral plants—were extensively used in Kyoto's gardens. Not that the entire garden was given over to them, but they were prominently placed, especially in the *senzai*, the "forward garden," that part built near the residence. *Senzai* had many forms (in fact the word referred to several things) but one ancient scroll shows the *senzai* as a collection of favorite plants, one specimen of each, planted in a small plot by a veranda: a tall grass that would hue bronze in autumn, a plum with scattered evanescent blooms (and three insect cocoons attached), and five or six perennial flowers. The plants were selected for their individual characteristics, not because they fit together to make a well-balanced, artistic arrangement. What's more, each plant individually expressed a mood: autumnal melancholy, evanescence of spring, and so on, and was chosen for the emotion it symbolized; a poetic understanding.

Some weeks ago, I stood in the middle of town at the intersection of Oike and Muromachi streets, a place that represents the antithesis of that understanding. Oike is a broad east-west avenue, one of Kyoto's largest; west of Muromachi it is lined with large, fifty-year-old zelkova trees that, like the grand elms of America and Europe, are tall and vase-shaped and arch over the street, turning it into a tunnel of filtered green light. They grant the street, though very wide, a comfortable scale and a tempered microclimate: the temperature a few degrees cooler, the wind less cutting, some air pollution filtered, a modicum of extra oxygen provided.

To the east of Muromachi, however, Oike is devoid of trees, the large zelkovas that once graced its sides having been stripped off in the process of building an underground parking garage. The garage was built as part of a project code-named "Symbol Road," because the mayor hoped the new street would become a symbol of "modern" Kyoto. His dream was to rival Paris's Champs Élysées, an affection for Western (rather than Asian) models surpassed only by his attempt to build a replica of a Parisian bridge,

Pont des Arts, over the Kamo River in an attempt to boost tourism to Kyoto. The Symbol Road project resulted in Oike Street being denuded and widened. Actually "widened" is incorrect. The street is now six meters less wide than the old street, but the dividers that once held the grand trees were removed, unifying the road into a single, massive swathe that *feels* wider. The intent was to increase the road's efficiency, but the effective result is an eight-lane sea of asphalt, a "Symbol Road" indeed, but not of the sleek "City of the Future" that its proponents hoped for; rather, it is a symbol of our dependency on automobiles and, more sadly, the ease with which we eliminate nature when it conflicts with other urban needs.

79

A bus rolled by, sunlight flashing off its windows, shimmering. I walked into the shade of the remaining trees and looked back at the barren street to the east, dreaming it anew, bordered by ranks of old trees. The trees, as I saw them, no longer had the evenly balanced shape of youth, but they had not been removed or replaced; in fact, to the contrary, the oldest among them had been hung with thick straw ropes, and in the shadows at their roots small dishes of salt and rice had been left as offerings. But this was no country shrine—city life continued around them. The street bustled beneath their shade, the sidewalks filled with people attending their business: going to meetings, shopping, talking on cell phones. A group of men and women were sitting about on boulders that had been placed on the street as benches, having an impromptu meeting, each nestling their own air-linked Think-Pad. When the group got up to leave, one among them walked over to a particularly old tree nearby whose form was now wizened and bent. The sidewalk curved away from its base to accommodate its thick roots. The woman clapped her hands together and made a short silent prayer before turning and running to catch her group. In my mind's eye, Oike Street was not a French-style boulevard (though those are beautiful in their own right) but rather resembled streets seen in old sepia photos of Japan lined with irregularly spaced, asymmetric old pines—irrational, organic, and divinely poetic—a street that, perhaps, a visitor from France might admire for its natural harmonies and thoughtfully mull as a model for his own city.

❀   ❀   ❀

Perhaps we need to be foolish, to ruin what we have in order to know its true worth. Perhaps we don't, and we're simply foolish to no end. Whichever, as we fumble our way through, we are not without landmarks or guidance. Beguiled by breezes, by movements in shadows, we are led to where the message lies in wait—at an ancient tree enfolded live within a hardened city, at a gnarled trunk slipping gracefully through a wall. I stand now by the old cherry, come here to know this place again, to reread its oracle and remember. Given neither entirely to the wild nor entirely to subjugation of that wilderness, the two together—nature and architecture—harmoniously intertwine, and elucidate the mystery . . . how to build, how to *be*.

LAYERS

LAST NIGHT IT WAS TOO HOT TO SLEEP; I LAY AWAKE, LOOKING through an open window at lightning in the sky sparking silently cloud to cloud, illumining wild, feral shapes. The light reflected off the face of my wristwatch lying near me on the tatami. With each flash, a fragmentary image of lighted clouds appeared momentarily on the crystal, then darkened, replaced by four precise phosphorescent dots marking the major hours, like points on a compass. FLASH! For a moment the lens went berserk—the electric chaos of thunderheads alive in the lens—then suddenly it was orderly again; a glowing second hand sweeping rational circles through time.

This morning, I rest in a temple garden, cool beneath an old wisteria arbor. Last night's sticky warmth falters, hesitant before a heavy blackness that gathers over the mountains to the north. The air cools and stirs, its pressure falling headlong; I can feel it in my joints. Above me, the leaves of the wisteria ripple in the breeze, flickering in waves across the arbor, off the edges, down between me and the temple pond in wind-tossed veils. The fluttering leaves seem to flow, but go nowhere. Like a mechanized image of a waterfall I once saw in a coffee shop, they cascade in place, fall, yet never reach the ground. The long, sweet-smelling panicles of flowers that hung in the arbor this spring have passed, leaving only their wiry stems, each studded with tiny nodules where petals were attached. The stems wave in the breeze the way willow branches do, supplely, whiplike. The dark clouds on the horizon gather in masses, but they are still distant; the sky just above is bright blue. The garden, its lotus pond blown with pink blossoms, swims in light.

Squeak, squeak, squeak! A little girl in a bright yellow dress comes running by, carefree. She has been circling the pond since she arrived with her mother. Squeak, squeak! She flies, running with arms outstretched like wings, her feet patting the ground, the sandals designed to make each step a squeak. In rapture, she delights at the wind on her face, the rhythm of her own feet, the light, the flowers. Her mother, who sits nearby, is slim, almost gaunt, long black hair falling loosely about her shoulders. She watches her daughter without smiling, her vision focused on something other than what lies at hand.

It's summer. Half the pond is choked with dull-green lotus leaves, large and disklike, floppy, with crenellated edges like elephant ears. They rise above the water surface, pointing in all directions, chaotic, layered one upon the next to form a dimpled mattress across the pond. I have a sudden desire to join the girl in her flight, to circle the pond with wings outspread, then leap out onto the lotuses and fall softly on their cushions, like Buddha dreaming.

The lotus is the flower of Buddhism; the pattern of its growth is perceived as an allegory for spiritual development. The plant grows in shallow, still water, the bottom of which inevitably becomes sedimented with silt and clay creating a deep, muddy ooze. Into that darkness, the lotus sends its roots—thick, chambered, and tubular. The bottom of the pond, viscous and dark, is symbolic to Buddhists of the mortal world we live in, its impurity and defilement. Yet, as lotus grow, they rise above that uncleanliness and push their splendid leaves high above the water surface, rising toward the light of heaven. Above the leaves, crooked stalks lift further still, each as thick as a thumb. At the end of each stalk is one large bud, acicular, like a hand held with all fingers squeezed into a point. Come summer, the bud unfolds into a flower so beautiful—the richness and shade of its color, the symmetry of its form—it has become an emblem of divine perfection. Buddhist lore proposes that even as the exquisite lotus rises to perfection from base origins, so too can we surmount our impure origins.

Yellow flashes across green; the girl flies by again, then stops, abruptly, looking into the pond. A flower herself, a perfect blossom aged four or five. Has she risen so quickly from the muck? Or, do we all begin as pure, only to fall at some point, lodge firmly in the mire, and need to work our way out again? The lotus describes a transition, an upward rising toward spiritual perfection, but it also represents a flow of time; the roots reach back into the past, the flower rises into the future. In bridging the distance, the lotus describes a continuity, a line (albeit crooked) that interpenetrates time.

Several hours south of here near Nara City there is a temple in which the entire garden describes a flow of time. Founded nearly a thousand years ago, the temple, called Jōruriji, sits in a shallow basin between low hills, a jewel in cupped hands. At the center of the temple is a large pond. To the west of the pond is a long, low wooden hall and to the east, on top of a small bluff, is a three-storied pagoda. The western hall, its weathered cedar structure now dark with age, contains nine sculptures of Amida Buddha; to the east, enshrined within the pagoda, is a sculpture of Yakushi Buddha. The choice of directions stems from Buddhist tradition which asserts that Amida Buddha presides over a western paradise called Saihō Jōdo, the Western Pure Land, and that Yakushi's paradise, Jōruri Sekai, the Land of Pure Lapis Lazuli, lies to the east. The placement of hall and pagoda express religious traditions as part of the landscape.

Yet, in addition to this spatial allegory there is also one of time woven into the garden. Yakushi is the Medicine Buddha, whose elixir alleviates and severs ties with past impurities, while Amida Buddha awaits those who are of pure heart and call his name sincerely, accepting them into the Pure Land and thereby removing them from the cycle of life and death. Yakushi in the past; Amida in the future. Pilgrims who come to the temple begin their prayers at the pagoda with appeals for salvation from past wrongdoings—then turn west, to face their futures.

❀   ❀   ❀

The girl is at the pond's edge now; her flights of fancy distracted by something that is floating in the pond: a flower petal. She is trying to use a stick to pull it to shore but can't quite reach it. Her mother sits in the shade of the nearby temple hall, contemplating the ground. I go over to the girl, catch the petal on the end of a stick and hand it to her. Her prize in hand, she smiles, looking it over, then to me says, "*Ageru, yo*," "Here, you take it," drops it, and flies away.

I stay; dallying at the water's edge, poking at the surface of the pond, probing its muddy depths, spinning out clouds of fine clay. Each twist of the stick stirs up another cloud and the feeling that I am tinkering with the past. I poke and recall a day when I was little, no older than the girl in the yellow dress, playing in my backyard, face down on the lawn. The grass has a warm summer smell; my mother's voice is nearby, calling softly. The cloud rises in the water and subsides. I push again and see a birth, my son slipping out from between his mother's legs, slick, red, arms and legs contracted against the sudden touch of cool air, and remember pausing in puzzled disbelief at seeing on his little body my own face. The cloud subsides. I poke again and am by the edge of a cold, wet highway at night. Nearby a battered car lies upside-down, a boy on the road, motionless, blood dripping from his ear, his father's head in my lap, he too not long to live. I stop there. Enough rummaging.

The clouds of mud settle, and as they do other clouds reflected in the surface of the water come into focus. The darkness of the pond bottom makes the surface mirrorlike; the sky hangs upside-down inside, a taut skin of light pinned across the pond. I glance up and down, comparing reality with illusion, and find the world in the water most alluring; there is a minute ripple to the reflection that gives it an added sense of motion not found in the real world. I throw the girl's petal back in the water. It floats away, pushed ever so slowly by the wind; a gossamer vessel plying the many worlds, real and reflected, that gather at the surface of the pond.

❀　❀　❀

The pleasure of sailing, I have come to realize (though, honestly, I am a sailor of little experience), is that it occurs on a surface where two fluid masses meet; sky and water. It is entirely different from walking, for instance, feet measuring clean, even steps against the solidity of the earth. Different, too, from flying or snorkeling in which you are immersed fully within air or water, given over entirely to their inclinations. When sailing you glide *between* the two, and the currents and urges of both affect you each in their own way; the wind draws you in a direction that one minute counters the intent of the water and the next amplifies it. In constant flux, wind and water move in vastly complex patterns that can be sensed but not determined, connected yet separate; the surface that lies between them is the sum of their changing moods. Sailing, you glide along that undulating plane, eye on the horizon, nudging the rudder, adjusting for changes in the surrounding fluid worlds. We live as if sailing, traveling the illusory surface that lies between past and future.

The present is an illusion. Like the glistening surface of a pond, it is a fictive layer between two worlds: a thing that appears to be, yet is not. The present marks the moment at which future flows to past, yet in the instant of its conception, it is already gone. The clouds reflected in the pond grow darker, each fold and ridge is real enough to touch yet completely unreal, existing only on an atom-thick surface that catches light and tosses it back; a mirror game. The root of the word mirror, *mirare*, means "to see" and similarly the root of miracle, *mirari*, means "wonder." It's not coincidental. Reflections hold wonders for those who look. A crow flies overhead, carried south on a tailwind. I see it reflected in the pond, traversing the cloud landscape; it wavers and dissolves in a drop of rain.

Another drop strikes a lotus leaf like a pea on a drum. Then another. Then many, shattering the clouds in the pond. I should run for cover (summer rains can turn torrential) but rain on lotus is a fascination beyond reason. I set my hat and settle in for a concert of sounds audible only at this spot, by a lotus pond in the rain. It comes slowly at first, rain pattering on leaves, then builds to a crescendo. The size and shape of each leaf determines its pitch; the hundreds gathered in the pond create a symphony. What's more, each leaf is somewhat cup-shaped and collects rain drop by drop. Microscopic hairs on the surface of the lotus leaf, which create its distinctive dull-green hue, also resist fluids, so that rain collecting on the leaf balls up, silvery, like liquid mercury. As the amount of water increases in size and weight, the leaf begins to sway on its stalk. The water rolls around lazily inside the hollow of the leaf, nearing the edge then slipping back to the middle, again and again, swaying drunkenly, until its weight overcomes the strength of the stalk and the leaf tilts and dumps the water into the pond. PLASH! Like frogs jumping. First one falls, then many. Raindrops patter, water plashes: music beyond notation.

❀ ❀ ❀

I stand under the eaves of the temple with the little girl and her mother, waiting out the rain. The pond trembles in the downpour. The girl sits on her mother's lap, face buried in her neck. Her mother stares out through the rain, gently stroking her daughter's hair. Something in her thoughts passes across her face like light, softening her brow, drawing a half-smile; then she retreats. She kisses the girl's hair and falls back to staring. I look away, pull an apple from my pack, and take a deep bite. A slight stinging arises on the inside edge of my lip, just at the point where the rough outer skin gives way to the wet inner lining of the mouth. Every time I feel this sensation, the same strange image comes to mind, that of a single human cell splitting.

Our embryonic development begins with a single cell that cleaves in two. Continuing, the two split to four, four to eight, and so on until a hollow sphere of a hundred or so cells is formed. The sphere then folds in upon itself forming a double-walled cup called a gastrula. The inner layer of the gastrula, the endoderm, will develop into the internal organs, the linings of the air passages, and digestive tract. The outer layer, the ectoderm, gives rise to our skin, hair, and fingernails. A third layer, the mesoderm, which forms between the other two, goes on to develop into our meatier parts—muscle, blood, and such. Three layers—that is where we start.

In Japan swords are made from layers of different types of steel, some harder than others. The swordmaster sits before an intense charcoal fire. He stacks small plates of steel one on top of the other, heats them until they glow, and then, while his assistants hold them tightly, he forges them with his hammer into a single block, sparks showering out from the work. Again he heats the steel, cuts it partway in two, and folds it, doubling the numbers of layers. Even though the master will repeat the process until the number of layers reaches into the thousands, the two metals do not completely blend. When he gives the sword its final shape and polishes it, the layers remain visible, creating on the sword a grain like wood. We too. Beginning with just a few embryonic layers, we are folded again and again upon ourselves in our mother's wombs, our complexity rising exponentially with each cleavage; as in swords, the primal layers repeated become the grain of our bodies, expressed within us forever.

I had always thought that the place that stings on my lip when I eat apples was the borderline between endoderm and ec-

91

toderm; that some strange quirk in the nature of that edge between inner and outer me, some small rent in the fabric of hu-
manity, allowed for the reaction. It turns out that the actual
threshold between those two worlds lies further in the mouth, at
the top of the throat, but I cannot eat an apple without seeing
cells dividing and envisioning the myriad folded layers of my
body. Looking back I see the little girl snuggle in against her mother sleepily, so close to the womb from which she came. She like a
lotus bud tight with petals; like a sword; layered.

＊　＊　＊

I spent some time with a friend last autumn in China, exploring
Xi Hu, West Lake, so named because it lies in that direction from
the center of Hangzhou city. West Lake was an object of fascination for Japanese gardeners throughout the eighteenth and nineteenth centuries, though none of them ever had the opportunity
to see the lake personally. They knew of it instead from references
in literature and from scenes in paintings. What caught the gardeners' fancy about the lake, and what they invariably incorporated into their gardens, was an earthen causeway that runs
across the lake, a slim spit of land, punctuated by several stone-
arch bridges, that traverses the watery plane like a single brush-
stroke on empty paper. In the Japanese gardens that employed the
causeway image, the original causeway was greatly reduced in size
to fit the constraints of smaller garden ponds in Japan. Not built
in miniature, instead abstracted, it was recreated as a small dike
containing two or three stone bridges—just enough to work as a
mnemonic device, triggering the flow of images ingrained

through education in the Chinese classics. As glyphs, the Japanese versions work well, but as an example of landscape art, it is the original that sings.

We arrived in Hangzhou at night, after a long, slow ride on the night-train from Shanghai, and woke in our hotel early the next morning. Decidedly bleary but none the less anxious to get out and about, I threw open the curtains to look outside. There was nothing: the window was chalk. A cold, heavy mist had settled on the city, shrouding the landscape, leaving only my own perplexed face staring back at me, dimly. It was like waking from a dream into a dream, not knowing, looking back at the bed expecting to see yourself asleep and finding instead only a warm impression left in the sheets.

We headed out an hour later. The air was still thick with fog and rich with the earthy scent of smoldering coal fires, white and motionless, no more than meters visible in any direction. As we walked down the hill to the causeway, the town materialized eerily before us: bicycles and cars, people ambling the sidewalks, large plane trees along the street. At first vague white apparitions, they gained form and color, grew believably real as they grew closer, emerging from the mist as if born of it, then slipped past and receded behind us into nothing: swallowed whole.

In addition to the causeway, there are several man-made islands in the lake that are accessible only by shallow gondolas. The dark-blue boats waited, dim by the pond's edge, still unmanned this early, the lake disappearing into the mist behind them. Launched into that white abyss, would they return or pass therein into another, as yet unknown, world?

Approaching the entry to the causeway, we could make out

its slim form stretching out into the lake, a long, narrow mound, low to the water, lined on both sides with rows of black trees, extending to infinity. It had no end. Instead, the land simply dematerialized in the distance, disappearing at the point where the mist and pale water fused, welded into a single block. We strolled some distance out the causeway. It was unearthly quiet, no other visitors, only the occasional bicycle appearing suddenly, humming by, and vanishing. By the time we got out to the first bridge, the shore had completely receded from view. All that was left was the ground beneath our feet, the trees close by, the water and the mist. The bridge arched high above the water to allow small boats to pass beneath. We walked up to the crest of the bridge and sat on its carved stone railing. Directly below, the water was the lustrous dull color of gunmetal, but looking out toward a distant shore we could not see, it gradually lightened in color, fading eventually to the hue of the mist, so that the line where sky and water met was imperceptible. No separation between past and future, we hung in the moment, adrift in a boundless present.

Later, we came upon a lotus plantation by the edge of the lake. Fenced in to keep the fish out, the shallows were massed with shriveled lotus stalks, an occasional tattered leaf tipped down to the water, frayed, punctured, browning along the edges. By then the mist had risen and reformed as low clouds that reflected in the water between the lotus. The brown stalks were bent and twisted, looking like rusted metal bars. Each stalk rose out of the water at an angle, bent over in half where it had weakened, and returned its seed-head to the water. Hundreds of those broken stems were reflected in the perfectly still, metallic surface of the lake, doubling, like crumpled wire set on a mirror. A half-circle above the water completed below; a triangle reflected into a rectangle; strangely twisted lines replicating, layering one upon the next, increasing in complexity toward the horizon, iterating to infinity.

The same lotuses that stretched so elegantly from root to bloom in summer now doubled back upon themselves, humbled and forlorn. When we idealize a linear flow of time from past through present to future, there is no symbol more graceful than the summer lotus, rising from muddy root to sky-bound bloom. Yet, if we were to trace our lives more realistically—our pasts in so many ways circling forward to affect our futures, resurfacing, re-fusing to be left behind—would it not look more like the snarled disorder of an autumn lotus field?

❀ ❀ ❀

The rain has passed. As quickly as it came, it went. Back at the water's edge, I sit on a wet rock and sketch the lotus from top down: open flowers; large ovate buds clasped in green; massed leaves, endlessly layered; and in the shadows beneath, green stalks tracing down into the water, receding into the darkness below. Down there, where sunlight pales, a slow current appears vaguely in the mud. It builds in strength and begins to move purposefully, out from the tangle of the roots toward me, rises, and assumes a form—a brown carp. Not one of the splendid varieties splashed with patterned colors; just a wild one, fat as Hotei, God of Good Fortune. It turns, lazily, spawning a cloud of silt with each stroke of its tail. Meandering back and forth, the fish slips in and out of the lotus' shadows: now here, now gone. Two dragonflies clatter into view, one clutching the other, reflected in the pond, silhouetted against clouds. They move in the staccato manner distinctive to their genus; hover, turn, rise and fall in short clean bursts, freezing in mid-air between each movement. Settling on the edge of a leaf, they hold still long enough for me to catch their gesture on paper, then swoop down to the water surface, making short neat dabs against the water, laying eggs, sending out a delicate ripple each time. The carp rises from below, floating up languidly, nearing the surface just as the dragonflies dip. Mouth near the surface, it sucks noisily, inhaling water, air, and insects indiscriminately, then sinks down and flows back into the shadows. Large ripples cast out across the water from where the dragonflies were, quicken, slow, and subside.

Things happen at surfaces: dragonflies meet fish; a boat tilts headlong with the wind; a memory lingers at the threshold of the present. We live in layers of time and space, some stretched taut, reflecting, some folded back upon themselves, convoluted, touching in places. The little girl in the yellow dress is leaving, asleep in her mother's arms. Something happened to make the woman so removed; something that is far away in time or space yet to which she is still inextricably linked, tugging at her from across a void, unwilling to let go. Was it long in coming, I wonder, or just a moment—a sudden death, a shock of betrayal—that broke surface, rippled, and now refuses to subside? The carp rises for another meal, but I'll not watch. I head for the gate, too, leaving that layer to be broken without testimony.

BALANCE

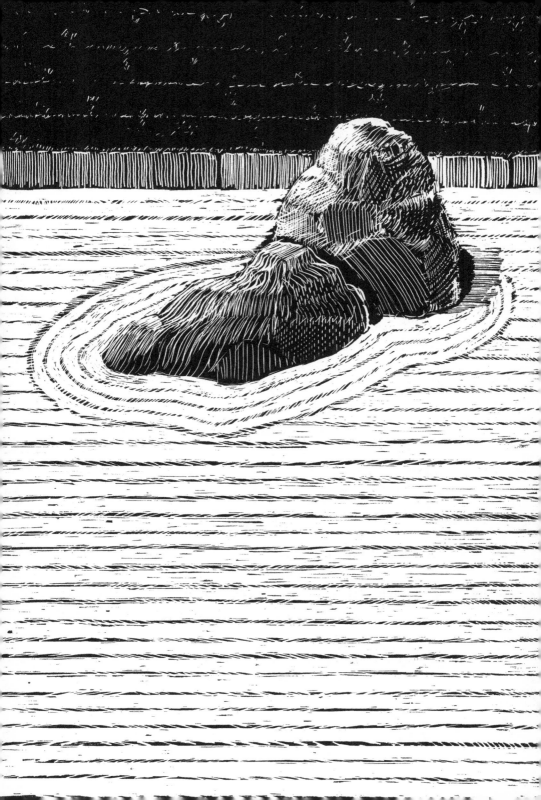

IN THE WEST OF KYOTO, FORESTS OF BAMBOO STRETCH FOR MILES across the hills and lowlands. Much of it is wild but some parts are tended as farms, neatly culled and cared for. This morning, on my way to a temple that has a simple rock garden, I rode down a narrow street that passed through one of the farms. Unlike forests of wild bamboo that become impenetrable mazes of standing and fallen culms, these farms are pristine. The land is terraced to make work easier and spread with a brick-red mountain soil for the iron it contains. The terraces continue for acre after acre, covered entirely with neatly spaced pale-green bamboo, repeating into the distance to the point where they blur, thousands upon thousands of clean vertical strokes. The forest was shot through with slim beams of angled light, illuminating a morning mist that lingered in the hollows. Something moved among them and I stopped to look.

Looking over a rough fence made of bundled bamboo branches, I saw an older man in loose gray clothes doing tai chi in a small clearing within the forest. He stood, by chance, just on the edge of a pool of soft light cast down amid endless half-shadow. His torso moved slowly, arms cutting gracefully through the air; inhaling, exhaling; pushing away, then drawing in; rising only to fall; circling endlessly, always in motion yet also in balance. It was a dance but not a performance; the movements were not intended to be seen but rather to be experienced by the dancer himself. Swaying back and forth slowly as if submerged in water, his face and chest slipped in and out of the shadows, alternately bathed in light, then absorbed into the dark background, at times revealed then hidden, appearing slowly again. I watched for a few minutes, increasingly caught up in his rhythms, mesmerized as by waves at the shore.

Something small and quick flashed among the bamboo close by, flitting from shadow to light and back. A song bird. It called out into the cool air: a short piercing note that cleared my thoughts like the stroke of a Zen master. In training temples, disciples gather each day for communal meditation, seated in neat rows, backs upright. Their masters pace behind them with upraised bamboo slats, ready to strike a quick smack across the shoulders of any who seem to be fading. The strokes are not dealt as punishment; they are meant to awaken, to refocus the disciple's meditation. They are received gladly; a single stroke at the right moment is believed capable of inducing enlightenment. The bird in the bamboo flickered and sang, each note awakening. I rode on, the tires of my bicycle humming a baseline to its melody.

Approaching the top of a small rise, the forest thinned, becoming lighter and warmer. I could see the gate of the temple in the distance below. It stood out clearly in the morning light, doors still bolted shut against the previous night. My bicycle picked up speed as it eased over the hill; air rustled about my jacket, sung in the spokes of the tires, and I rode gravity all the way to the gate, losing the last bit of energy gained from the hill just as I coasted quietly up alongside the temple wall where I stand now, waiting on the hour. A bell strikes, and I walk to the gate.

❀   ❀   ❀

The temple gate is a grand wooden structure many times my height, roofed with heavy tiles, weathered from years of exposure. Pushing open the small side door that stands off to the right of the main gate, I duck inside quietly. The sound of sweeping comes from further within. Following it, I find a young acolyte tending the garden as part of his morning chores. He is dressed in dark blue garb made of rough cotton and has a thin white towel tied neatly around his shaved head. I call out softly. He turns, offering a bow and quiet greeting in return. For him, the sweeping of the garden is not so much a chore as a form of religious practice, what Zen priests call *samu*. Each morning for the last three days I have come here before the temple's normal opening hours to have time alone with the garden. Founded nearly five hundred years ago, the temple has been tended with care over the centuries, but only came into its own as a tourist attraction since the end of the last World War. Although it was supported in the past by wealthy provincial lords, it now seeks alms from another source, one that arrives each morning by the busload. The young priest-in-training and I talk briefly, then he turns back to his work and I head inside.

Entering a large earth-floored hall that formerly served as a kitchen for the temple in the days when twenty or thirty young acolytes lived here communally with the elder priests, the low sound of chanted prayers comes from further within: rhythmic, droning, accompanied by a quick beating on a wooden gong. The musky scent of incense hangs in the air, impregnated from years of use into the very walls and floors of the old building. Shoes off and set aside on a shelf, I take a long step up from the earthen floor to the smooth wood floor and head down a corridor that leads to the main hall, the songs of the priests fading behind me. There I find a wide veranda, protected beneath a broad overarching eave but opened fully to the garden alongside it, an intermediary space that is neither outside nor in, but hangs in the balance between garden and architecture. The veranda is on the southern side of the main hall, which enshrines an image of the founder of the temple. All is quiet, the distant chanting reduced to barely a hum.

The garden that the veranda faces is abstract—only sand and stones. It is bright, rectangular, and dry, warming quickly in the sun. The rooms facing it, though open to the light of the garden, recede within into shadow. From them flows a chill air that slips across the wooden floor. Entering, I pay respects to the statue of the founder in a curtained alcove, light incense sticks in his memory, and stand them in a pot of ash set on the low altar in front of his image, then turn and sit facing the garden. Seen from within the shadows of the room, the garden glows; it is almost too bright to look at. All the sliding doors along the outside of the hall have been removed, as they are each morning, offering a view of the garden obstructed only by an occasional slim, squared, wooden post. From inside the room, the garden looks like a scroll painting unfurled horizontally; the stones in white gravel appear as dabs of ink on paper.

Surrounding the garden is a low earthen wall, rough and patched in places, like the wall I wrote of earlier, with the cherry slipping through it. This wall, however, is not capped with tile but with a broad roof made of cedar bark. In the earliest days of the temple, this space was simply an empty courtyard used as a formal entrance to the main hall. But sometime during the sixteenth century a simple stone garden was built within it.

There may have been a time when the court served both functions—entrance and viewing garden—for the stones were set carefully so that they do not obstruct the path that would have

103

existed between a gate, which used to stand at the east side of the court, and a set of stairs that used to lead up from the garden to the center of the main hall. This dual use may have also influenced the sparsity of its design: just nine stones set in a bed of fine gravel. A more complex design would have gotten in the way of those entering. The stones were not placed evenly within the garden but rather were set in clusters, and between them lies nothing but gritty sand and empty space.

I sit. Time slips by easily, expanding. The sound of my own breathing becomes increasingly apparent, audible from within as when under water, resonating soothingly inside the ear. The shape of the courtyard becomes strikingly clear, its simplicity alluring, like clear water. The stones, form in void, break the stillness, initiating echoes that have a fascination of their own. They punctuate the emptiness of the garden as unmistakably as the cry of a songbird pierces the silent forest; their presence astounds no less than a sharp slap on the back.

As I sit with the garden, each stone begins to occupy a place within a mental map, the forms of the stones transcribed as other senses—a sound, a touch. As if played on a bamboo flute, the stones describe a rhythm: three clear notes, a brief pause in which the breath is heard breaking across the edge, five more, and then a silence that is drawn out to an impossible length, followed by a final quick blast.

A small bird drops out of a tree beyond, skims the crest of the wall, and cuts across the garden, wings flickering black and white toward the back of the temple. I get up and follow, heading back out to the veranda and around to the northern side of the hall. As I turn the corner, the sound of running water comes from a small, overflowing stone laver into which water is being fed through a slim bamboo pipe. The bird is nowhere to be seen.

The two sides of the temple, north and south, are different in character, defined by their original functions in the era of the temple's founding. The southern half was the outward face of the temple, the *hare* side, while the northern was the inward face, the *ke* side. In the past, the head priest would meet with his patrons and other important guests in the southern half of the hall, entertaining them by the austere dry garden, its formality appropriate for the purpose. The northern half, comprising smaller rooms, was the priest's residence and study, and the garden outside was for his pleasure.

Although the rooms, both north and south, are much the same architecturally—the walls made of clay, the floors covered with tatami mats—certain aspects of the rooms were embellished to reflect their divergent functions. Most notable were the themes of the paintings on the paper doors that enclosed the rooms. While the southern rooms featured gorgeous paintings of fantasy tigers prowling groves of bamboo rendered in lapis lazuli and black ink on pure gold foil, the paintings in the private northern rooms were austere black and white ink landscapes or portraits of Chinese philosophers of bygone eras. Those of the southern half strove to impress, the northern to instill a reflective mood.

The gardens to the north and south were different as well, and still are today. While one is dry, spread with granular sand, the other is moist, shaded, and quilted in moss. One is framed neatly into a crisp rectangle; the other segues imperceptibly into the forested hillside. One utilizes a palette of mineral earthtones—beige clay walls, russet brown stones, and white sand—the other is all botanical, dyed deeply in a chlorophyll green that vibrates from the moss and reflects among the maples and camphors in the wood beyond. One bathed in light, formal, outward, and social; the other mellowed by shadow, introspective, connected as directly with the forest as the society of man.

The main hall and its gardens are arranged to north and south harmonically like equal weights across a fulcrum. Though the materials of each differ, and their intention and aesthetics, the two halves together form a whole and balance each other in a gentle equilibrium of philosophy.

The stone laver overflowing with water is within easy reach of the veranda. On top of it lies a small bamboo ladle. Taking a single scoop of clear water, I rinse my hands and mouth. It tastes like the mountain. The excess tipped from the ladle falls without a sound on a tuft of moss, which absorbs it and deepens in hue. I slide open the door to one of the private chambers, no longer lived in, and, leaving the door partly open so that the garden remains visible, sit in the middle of the room, waiting for my eyes to adjust to the dim light.

Slowly the painting on the doors becomes visible as if appearing out of a mist—a fitting illusion, since the painting is of mist-shrouded mountains. The scene is Chinese, yet it is a landscape no person has seen, a fantasy by a medieval painter in Kyoto dreaming of faraway China, the source of all "modern" knowledge at the time. What the artist drew was derived from literature and paintings imported from the mainland, the way the image of West Lake was imported, but the particular shape he lent it was entirely his own. At the bottom of the painting, which stretches across four panels, a man poles a small boat along a narrow river through a mountain ravine. On either side of the river, cliffs rise abruptly, thrusting upwards into layers of mist where they disappear. Above the mist are seen the tops of mountains but they too hover in clouds, some peaks revealed, others lost. From high within the mountains, a waterfall plunges through empty space to the river below in a series of long cascades, riding gravity.

The artist painted with a fine-tipped brush in short quick strokes of black ink. In particular, the place where the cascade pounds against the rocks, the details of the boat and its cargo, and the edges of the mountains that rise above the river are, on close inspection, no more than a series of feathery strokes. The mist that the water plummets through, however, like the clouds that conceal the mountain tops, was not expressed with ink but rather by leaving the white paper untouched, an emptiness that is as potent as the painted image itself.

Many years ago, as part of a seminar in art history I took part in an experiment in understanding balance as applied to classical Renaissance paintings. Each of the students was given black and white copies of certain masterpieces and asked to draw four slender red lines through them, two vertically and two horizontally, dividing the page evenly into nine parts. The paintings, we found, were balanced on those divisions, organized in a measured, calculated way around the interfaces of the nine squares. In a Botticelli depicting Christ's death, the arms of two mourners cascaded down the left side of the central box, Christ's white legs formed the bottom, his body, supported from behind, rose up the right side, and the faces of anguished women carried across the top, completing the central square. In a Rembrandt, Abraham's face, gazing astonished at an angel who stills his murderous hand, fell precisely behind two intersecting red lines, like a deer caught in cross-hairs.

The balance of thirds lent an order and an air of repose to those paintings. In contrast, the paintings on the doors in this temple are wildly "off-balance," at least, by Renaissance standards. Large areas are left blank as mist and clouds. The focal points—the man poling down the river, the waterfall, a hermit's hut high atop a mountain—fall far off center, certainly nowhere near the intersection of golden thirds.

The temple's gardens are designed with the same sense of "off-balance" balance, especially the one to the south of the hall, with its sparsely set stones, an understandable coincidence since the men who designed gardens when this garden was built were also often painters, and the aesthetics applied to the creation of the one were also applied to the other. The asymmetric placement of the stones lends the garden a dynamic visual movement—a potential energy derived from the imbalance—but, of course, all energy derives from imbalance.

Perfect balance engenders entropy, a state of non-energy. The ancients in China perceived this and used it thousands of years ago as the basis for their theories of universal physics. They postulated that the cosmos began in a state of pure entropy that they called *wuji*, or non-polarity: no hot and cold, no light and dark, no energy and matter. All is All; All is One. It was not a nihilist condition, a Great Void, but rather a state of perfect balance that is incomprehensible to us. Living in a world of contrasts and made of differential material ourselves, we are not equipped through our experiences to grasp the reality of a completely unified world.

According to the theory, at some point in the distant past there was an epochal event at which the unified cosmos divided into two separate, opposing, yet complementary parts: Yin and Yang. As this theory was applied to understanding the world, each part was associated with certain natural elements: Yin with night, the moon, winter, north, and things feminine; Yang with day, the sun, summer, south, and things masculine. What's more, each pair (dark and light, male and female, and so on), though opposites, was believed to exist only in relation to the other, as separate facets of a single thing. In reality, all manner of natural things contain aspects of both Yin and Yang, though rarely in equal proportions. The classic symbol of Yin and Yang, familiar now to many, is a circle composed of two parts, one black, the other white, each shaped like a bent teardrop, nestled one against the other inside the circle. The symbol represents an endless cycle; as the white tear grows fatter the black recedes, then the black expands consuming the white, one continually replacing the other in a cycle of growth, extinction, and rebirth.

What's more, Yin and Yang are not depicted as separate entities. On the black teardrop, there is a small white dot, and vice versa: Yin within the Yang, Yang within the Yin. The teardrop shapes are described as being Old and the dots as being Young. Within the teardrop representing Old Yin is a dot of Young Yang and within Old Yang is a dot of Young Yin. Old is another way of saying *climaxing;* a thing in its fullest, while Young means *incipient*, something about to come into being. What the icon describes visually is that within the Old (a thing having risen to its fullest), there exists a fragment of the Young (an emergent seed) waiting to unfold and replace its host. The world in all its parts, large and small, is in flux—a perpetual imbalance—developing, climaxing, extinguishing, birthing again; opposites in synchrony, spiraling endlessly about each other, like the hands of a tai chi dancer.

Outside, to the rear of the garden, the pendulous branches of a large weeping cherry tree sway like long strands of kelp in an ocean current. The winds that gentle the cherry, like the currents in surf, are also the result of an imbalance, in this case an imbalance of heat. Hot areas in the atmosphere and in the oceans expand and spiral outward; cold ones contract. The result is wind and currents. Some spiral horizontally, others cycle vertically. Invisible columns of warm, moist air rise off the earth from sun-heated ground and billow up through cooler air until they hit a layer cold enough to condense them. The ensuing droplets of water collect by the billions and cumulus clouds appear, those puffs of aerial cotton-candy on which we projected our childhood dreams: a bear, a rabbit, a clipper ship bound for distant shores. Each cloud marks the point where a column of air is rising (or was rising), while the cooler air around the clouds, displaced, falls back to earth, a constant vertical cycle driven by an imbalance of heat.

This imbalance of heat can in turn generate an electric imbalance. The water droplets and ice crystals in the clouds collide and lose electrons, negative charges, resulting in positive and negative ions. The negative ions collect at the bottom of the cloud; the positive ions are carried on up to the top, over time forming a massive energized field, a fluffy magnet of immense proportions, hovering in the sky. When the cloud's downward facing negative field is strong enough to affect the ground, it pushes free electrons away from the surface further into the earth, negative repulsing negative. In losing its electrons, the surface of the earth becomes positively charged; above it hangs the negative side of the cloud's energy field. The imbalance has peaked; only milliseconds awaits the strike.

The attraction between negative cloud and positive earth—celestial Yin and terrestrial Yang—draws electric tendrils out from both. From objects on the earth, positively charged electrical streamers stretch up into the sky a short distance and wait. From the cloud, negatively charged streamers called step leaders probe through the air, ionizing it, seeking a path to connect cloud to earth. The leaders jump in surges, unevenly, leaping along the path of least resistance, following impurities in the air that act as stepping stones. Of the many step leaders descending from the cloud, one will reach a streamer first and in that instant, WHAM, the whole system—primary leader, secondary leaders, and cloud alike—dumps its excess electrons back into the earth. The infinitesimal negative charges that rose atom by atom in streams of gaseous water, and gathered in clouds like steam on glass, now gush back home in unison, burning plasma tubes through space, exploding the very air. It is the heat of the electron rush we see, the shock wave of the ensuing explosion we hear: a sensory understanding of a momentary event by which an imbalance adjusts itself.

Lightning is awe-inspiring but it is too swift and erratic an imbalance to make practical use of. Still, the energy we use to drive our societies comes from tapping into imbalances of one form or another: falling water turns a water wheel with the energy imparted it by an imbalance of height; huge aluminum propellers on white masts turn languidly on bluffs overlooking the sea, whooshing dully as they extract the energy conferred to the wind by the imbalance of heat; steel turbines embedded deep inside a dam stretched across the mouth of a harbor spin in one direction with the rising tide and in the other with the ebb, providing electricity either way, driven by an imbalance of lunar origin.

The examples are endless and yet, despite the abundance of imbalances that nature provides us with, we are not always satisfied. Because the natural sources were not always available when we needed them, or where we needed them, we began to make our own imbalances, beginning by raising water behind dams to artificially create an imbalance of height. Another artificial imbalance created for the energy it provides is the chemical battery. Not just a source of electricity (electrons), it is an electrical pump that sends free electrons into a wire, collects them after they have done their work, and shuffles them over to be used again. All this relies on an imbalance inherent to the materials within the battery. The negative side, the anode, is made of a material that has a tendency to lose one or more of its electrons while the positive side, the cathode, in reverse, can accept free electrons into its molecular structure. A tendency to give, a tendency to receive. The electrons flow from anode to cathode because of that imbalance.

The imbalances we create, though they serve us well in some ways, often come home to roost. Who threw the first logs across a river to feed a sluice is long forgotten, but nowadays the Chinese, who so long ago teased the riddle of Yin and Yang out of their natural world, are now proposing to throw a wall across the Yangtze to create an imbalance of unprecedented proportions, one that will instigate a thousand other imbalances, social as well as ecological.

❀   ❀   ❀

The sunlight in the room dims and strengthens as clouds pass overhead. The mute painted mountains that surround me seem to waver, rising then receding; the mist drifts through the valleys, the waterfall tumbles. I slide the door open and go back out to the veranda, continuing around the hall to the southern side again.

One usually walks around these halls clockwise. Not prescribed; just customary. Most pilgrimages are done in that direction: tourists strolling around a temple hall; *kinhin*, the slow, rhythmic walk Zen priests take between sessions of *zazen*, seated meditation; even a three-month excursion around an entire island traveling from temple to temple. Perhaps it's a northern hemisphere phenomenon, a Coriolis effect on humans, moving us in the same direction that hurricanes swirl or that water twists down a drain.

Turning the corner toward the light of the southern garden, I hear the sound of rattling glass from the entry hall down the corridor; a window is being opened in the reception office. Within an hour the first of today's buses will arrive, brimming with eager visitors. They come for different reasons: to discover their history, for spiritual refreshment, perhaps simply to inherit a small portion of the timeless air of the temple. Whatever the reason, the thing they seek is lacking wherever they come from, an absence that sets them on their journey. They will come; they will pay. That is the economic reality of this temple these days. Economics can be viewed as a means of explaining the flow and inter-action of various energies, both material and social, and even as energy is derived from imbalance, so are economies.

Economies begin with a natural imbalance, an inequality in concentration of materials or services, or in the way those things are valued. Supply and demand. A spice grows plentifully on a far-away island and is desired by people who live on the other side of the world where the climate prohibits its growth. Before a route connecting the two places is established, a potential economy ex-ists, like the potential energy of water pooled on a mountain top, or that latent within an unconnected battery. Complete the route, however—by ship or caravan or overnight delivery—and an economy proceeds, the way chemical reactions in a battery begin when their polar nodes are connected by a wire. In a battery, the energy will flow as long as the anode releases electrons and as long as the cathode can absorb them, but batteries lose their power as free electrons are locked up in a more stable form. Likewise, economies wear themselves out.

A battery drains instantly when short-circuited by a wire at-tached directly from anode to cathode. Similarly, if the mecha-nism of delivery in an economy is overly successful, the destination will be flooded with a product, or the source of the product will be depleted, resulting in a state of economic entropy. This sudden rush could be described as "lightning economics." The forests of Brazil and Indonesia fall to provide cheap wood to the world. The flow is strong; too strong. In a flash (milliseconds on an ecological scale), the forests are clear-cut, while in the countries on the receiving end, the massive scale of the imports wreaks havoc with local timber economies. The flow is powerful but destructive. Lightning economics. Like cloud and ground; on one end depletion, on the other, something gets burned.

Just as we are not always satisfied with the imbalances that nature provides us with for physical energy, so it is with our economies. Wanting them to be where we want them, when we want them, for as long as we want them, we foster and subsidize them; in short, we cultivate economic imbalances. We hoard resources, releasing them in careful doses to maintain an imbalance (oil comes to mind); we create imbalances of desire through advertising (all the things we are taught to believe we cannot do without); we maintain or foster social inequalities to benefit from the imbalance of labor costs (this being the most insidious).The logical, chilling conclusion is: since the forces that drive a mercantile economic system are based on imbalances, it is fundamentally and inherently impossible within a mercantile economy to obtain an equal distribution of wealth.

❀ ❀ ❀

The garden stones are calming; their mute presence somehow reassuring. I sit on the veranda to be closer to them the way one will sit at the edge of the ocean, not needing to enter to be refreshed. The stones cast shadows, marking out dark crescents on the sand. They are brown, but not uniform in color—some rust, others coffee, all gnarled and angular. They have been set out in space to develop a tension, an imbalance that gives the garden its visual vitality, like the positioning of the mountains in an ink landscape, scattered about in the mist. Though many explanations have been attributed to the garden over the years, the meaning remains unclear. Still, an inherit understanding of the potency of imbalance applies, even as it does to the ink landscape paintings that served as models for the garden's design. The natural world has provided many symbols and motifs for artists—plum blossoms to express evanescence, running water to reveal nature's constant flux—but the landscape itself supplies the most compelling philosophy, a single, potent thought. Imbalance is energy.

Even though the parts of nature are animated by minor imbalances, the total of those imbalances aggregate into a system that is in balance, the way the gardens on the northern and southern halves of this temple do. Yin releasing into Yang, Yang sustaining Yin; always slightly out of kilter, always in accord. Something may prove to be out of balance on the micro scale yet it participates at a larger scale in a system within which it is in balance, thus providing for its own continuation. If it is not somehow balanced at the macro scale it will not be around for long. If there is any definition for the word "natural" it is that—wholistic balance.

When we look at something natural that pleases aesthetically—the pendulous curve of a branch, waves rolling at sea, this temple garden of only stones and sand—we find small-scale imbalances that animate it and make it dynamic and attractive. But at the same time we find the object expresses an inherent large-scale balance (it must if it is truly "natural") that we instinctively respond to, that puts us at ease, is somehow reassuring. Surely the beauty of this garden stems from the combination of the two: a delicate interplay of stillness and energy.

The imbalances that foster energy in nature, that power our societies and drive our economies, are distilled in this garden into just a few stones, held in tension across a field of raked white sand. And, like batteries that flow only when connected or spice that is ascribed a value only when linked to those desirous of it, so the imbalance in the garden activates and begins to flow only when observed . . . by us. It is we, at the veranda's edge or in the shadows of the room nearby, who complete the link and turn the potential energy of the garden into reality, and to our delight we find the wellspring endless. We drink our fill in peace, steady in our faith it will not run dry. Unlike chemistry or economics, the energy of art is provided without loss to itself.

117

The bird reappears from behind the temple and alights on the top of the furthest stone. It bobs up and down, tail pumping. One eye turns to me. It freezes, holds, then presses its chest forward and releases a long sweet note: crystal clear, piercing.

THE ART OF SETTING STONES

THE SUN IS SLOW TO SHOW TODAY. SLENDER GRASSES ALONG THE garden path remain fringed with frost, showing russet, tan, and burgundy beneath a delicate lace white. Beneath them, pale-yellow ginkgo leaves lie scattered by the hundreds with more in drifts by the house, blown off the tree and under the eaves by last night's wind. A large stone waits slightly tilted by the path that leads behind the house. At the end of the path, amid piles of tools, three gardeners huddle over an old iron can: an elder man, thin and wiry, his gray hair clipped tight, and two young assistants, fuller and taller than he. Small puffs of breath whiten in the chill air as I walk over to where they are. I pat the stone affectionately in passing.

Gardeners have their rituals, like breaks for tea at ten and three, and on chill mornings a fire always precedes the beginning of work. As I enter the circle, white smoke rises from a small pile of twigs in the can, flames lick through the wood, crackling. The warm glow bathes outstretched hands, flickers across faces. We shuffle and clap, sip tea from thermoses, talk eagerly about nothing. One of the young men picks up a handful of loose twigs, snaps them in two. Some spicebush must have been mixed among them—a sudden sweet scent hinting of cinnamon mixes with the woody smoke.

We have been working together for the last few days, building a small garden in front of a sitting room recently added to the side of an old home. Last year, clearing space for the new construction, we removed part of the old garden, saving what we could reuse and selling the rest to others in the trade. In Japan, garden materials—plants, stones, lanterns, and the like—make rounds through gardens like bees at flowers, and though their

journey is less fleet, like them they occupy any one spot only temporarily. Those that remain in place for centuries are rare; most
are destined by the vagaries of history to a more transient life.
The boulder waiting by the path is like that. It had been in the
garden of a merchant's house for many generations before coming to this garden; and that was over seventy years ago. When we
dismantled the old garden, we took it out, temporarily, and the
construction of the new one will begin by putting it back: a link
from old to new. Today we hope to set it in place but it is large,
perhaps too big for even four of us, and we linger by the fire,
glancing at it from time to time as if to measure its weight. We
talk some more, the fire grows hot, then wanes. A break in the
clouds sends pools of light skimmering down the garden path,
sparkling in the grasses by the stone. Now only the last embers
glow. Time to work.

To carry the stone we use a sturdy wooden pole and a length
of strong rope doubled over itself. The rope wraps the stone,
which hangs from the pole we carry on our shoulders, like prey
slung home by hunters. Two in front, two in back, we crouch,
place the pole on our shoulders and lift to the measure of a
rhythmic count. As the stone rises, the pole cuts into our necks,
painfully, the weight not simply heavy but magnetic, the desire of
the stone to return to the earth channeled directly through the
muscle and bone of our bodies. We move forward a few steps and
stop to rest. This needs to be done in stages.

Once again, the old gardener calls out and we lift, leaning
into the pole, thrusting our weight against it to prevent it from
sinking. I hear bells, see flashes of black and gold, swaths of white
blurring in motion. The pole presses deeper into my shoulder,

cutting in. The smell of sweat and saké comes strongly, awakening a memory.

It is dusk. Fifty men are gathered at the *otabisho*, a communal place in a Japanese village something like a New England green, only here it is brown, a sand-covered courtyard used through most of the year for agricultural chores: cleaning and drying vegetables, threshing rice, repairing tools. The court is surrounded by several old wooden buildings including a low hall where the neighborhood gathers for meetings, and a large storehouse, its high doors now thrown wide open. Fires burn in iron baskets around the perimeter of the court, casting rippled light across the sand, on the walls of the buildings, the overhanging trees, and the people gathered there. We have just carried out of the storehouse a large portable shrine called a *mikoshi*, an elaborate, two-ton construction like a miniature house finished in shiny black lacquer, complete with swinging doors and a curved, gilt roof. It rests now in the court outside the storehouse, set high on stands, gleaming in the firelight. Lashed beneath it are two sturdy wooden beams that taper at the ends, each broader around in the center than two hands can measure, over thirty feet in length, allowing it to be carried like a royal palanquin.

We mill about, anxious to get started. Half-naked, what little we wear—cloth boots, shorts, open jackets—is white, a symbol of purity. We have gathered for the annual autumn festival to carry the *mikoshi* around the neighborhood, up to the main shrine and back. The purpose of the ritual is purification, to receive the blessing of the gods. Gradually we line up, taking our places along the beams, staggered right and left along them. When ready, each man shoulder to beam, a signal to lift is given.

With a communal grunt, we heave the shrine to our shoulders, circle the court once, and head out to the street. As we leave the *otabisho*, the glow of the fires gives way to the glare of streetlights, cold and brittle in comparison. They hang above our heads from concrete utility poles, linked through webs of black cable to a synchronous current pulsing sixty times per second, across the neighborhood, across the city—the heartbeat of the nation. We shoulder the *mikoshi* among those wired poles as ancestors did through forests. We call the same coarse chants to brace ourselves but they echo not from trees, only from cinderblock walls. A cold misty rain begins to fall and the streets turn slick, streaked with electricity.

We make our way noisily through the backstreets toward the main shrine, chanting, passing among our neighbors lined up outside their houses, reveling in their praise, drinking freely of the saké they offer. The *mikoshi* is decorated with bells that ring dully and loose metal plates that jangle when shaken. Whenever we muster the energy, we stop our march and shake the *mikoshi* feverishly, rocking it wildly on our upheld arms. Our chant grows louder, sharpened by wildly clattering bells. The gods awaken and take notice.

To carry a *mikoshi* properly, its bearers must lean in against the supporting beams sideways, not push up from underneath, so that the combined mass of their bodies forms a series of triangles, spreading the *mikoshi*'s massive weight through them to the ground. If more were to push right then left, the *mikoshi* would slide off the road, yet that doesn't happen. Like fish schooling, the bearers form an organic mass—lacking a single brain, yet guided by some other sense—and the *mikoshi* lurches forward.

Earlier, when no one was looking, I tried to lift it by myself. Crouching, I put my shoulder to the wooden arm, and heaved upward. There wasn't the slightest give. Yet later, when we all gathered, untrained but willing, excited by the night and camaraderie, braced with *saké*, we lifted to the call of an elder and the *mikoshi* rose as if levitated . . . responding not to I but to We. Not I but We.

Several thousand years ago, the idea of growing rice in paddies was introduced to Japan from elsewhere in Asia; perhaps Korea or China—perhaps from further south. The technique seemed simple. Flatten the land and border it with low dikes, flood it in spring, plant seedlings, harvest in the fall. In fact, it was arduous, time-consuming work. Encoded in the written character for "rice" is a glyph for the number "eighty-eight"—traditionally the number of tasks required to bring rice from seed to table. The difficulties of rice farming, especially the intricacies of irrigation, are enormous. It is work for We not I. But despite the hardship, the system worked, providing stable food for many. Hamlets blossomed, squeezed between the flatland and the mountains, the former increasingly developed for rice production, the latter too steep to build on. Living in the tight physical constraints of the hamlet, and dependent on each other for help in the fields, a strong communal spirit was fostered among the early farmers.

❀   ❀   ❀

We lurched forward in the night rain, drenched and drunk; alternately dancing in place, tossing the *mikoshi* to shake a rhythm from its metallic filigree, then slogging slowly a little further through the streets toward the shrine, numbed by our own exertion. Realizing my utter inability to do what we were doing alone, the purpose of the ritual—the reason for all the sweat and pain— became suddenly clear. An affirmation of community, of its power and ensuing pride. As we four stumble forward now, weighed down by this garden stone, I can't help but wonder if that isn't also the point of setting stones in gardens. Their inherent weight necessitates the work of many—transporting them draws us together in a common goal—so their very existence in the garden stands as testament to our community.

127

We pause again. The younger two light up cigarettes, drawing deeply for nicotine. The old gardener pulls the scarf from his neck and wipes his face and hair. He catches me looking at him and we smile, both caught in this endeavor, enjoying it despite the effort. We sit sprawled about the stone, framing it like the petals of a flower. The stone waits on us, its face to me, bowed forward slightly as if questioning. An odd word, "face," to use about a stone, but that is what gardeners say. A stone's face is the side with the best attributes, the one that is directed toward the front of the garden. They call the top of the stone "heaven," but in the past it was called the "head." Heads and faces, an animistic view of nature applied to stones that began long ago amid the shadows of the forest.

In ancient times, all of nature was perceived as animate. The *Nihon Shoki*, a chronicle of Japan's antiquity, records a time in the distant past, called the Age of the Gods, when "the trees and grasses had the power of speech," a phrase that does not imply that the plants were actually talking but that the people of that time were attuned to the intricacies of nature, able through that intimacy to gain knowledge pertinent to their lives, even from the most common of things: a blade of grass, the blossoms on a tree. Of that vast, animate world, some things were held sacred and deified accordingly: waterfalls and clear springs where life-giving water flowed inexplicably from solid ground; massive trees whose girth and height inspired reverence; boulders, their solidity a manifestation in miniature of the mountain that bore them. Not every tree, or flow of water, or stone was chosen, only those in which a spiritual aura was perceived.

There is a sacred boulder not far from where the *mikoshi* is stored. Though forgotten now, it was the focus of prayer long before the *mikoshi* was carved and gilded, before shrine buildings were conceived of, even before the advent of farming, in a time when the people of this valley lived within the wild, collecting what they could along with those with whom they shared the land—the bears, deer, and hawks. The sacred stone was not a deity to them, but rather was believed to be a conduit through which the gods of nature could be approached, enticed from their abode in high places—mountaintops and clouds—to join the circle of man. Entreated through prayer and sacred gifts, the gods could, they believed, be drawn to the stone and, through it, accepted into another object by which they could be transported to the village nearby. The vessel used was elegantly simple . . . an evergreen branch.

The first time I saw the sacred stone was by accident, in summer a few years ago. My five-year-old son and I were out on a walk to our favorite overlook at the top of a hill nearby our home. It was, as I remember, a very hot day, the kind when the glow of heat from asphalt streets is palpable. From our house we made our way down treeless streets, the tangled powerlines, despite their numbers, doing little to relieve the heat, their shadows mocking, playing across our shoulders as we walked. Ducking into the shadows of a narrow lane between two wooden apartments, just to get out of the sun, we stopped for a quick drink of water. Pouring a cool cupful from a thermos for the boy, I noticed behind him a strong green light at the end of the lane, so after we finished, we headed on down that way to see what it was. The lane led to a hidden enclave of fields at the back of the buildings, alive with the energetic green of summer rice. Beyond the fields were the low hills to which we were heading. I could see that the overlook was just up the slope in front of us and was tempted to try a new route.

We took a dirt path that arced in a broad curve between the fields to the forested hill and headed up a set of roughly built steps on the hillside. Entering the forest, we were met by a cool breeze and the insanely loud whirring of mate-seeking cicada in the trees. Soon we found that the path led only to a small graveyard where an elderly couple were tending a plot, arranging flowers, splashing the gravestone with water to offer respite from the heat to the spirits within. They looked up silently; we exchanged bows. The graves were surrounded by forest, no paths leading further on. But, the hill in front of us wasn't very high; I figured we could find our way through so we pushed straight on into the brush. Trying to avoid low branches, pull my son along, and keep my own balance on the steep slope, I found myself walking bent over, face down, and so halfway up the hill nearly smacked right into the stone before seeing it: a large boulder, pushing out of the soil. Twice my height, the stone was completely enclosed by low scrub trees, its shaded base covered in moss, but the remnants of a small wall in front of the stone hinted at the cleared sacred space that would have existed around it when it was the object of active prayer.

In the nineteenth century, French archeologists stumbled across Angkor Wat, an immense Buddhist temple in the jungles of Cambodia. It was hidden, encrusted by the thick roots of trees that appeared to flow down the stone edifice like ice-falls on a glacier. As the significance of what they had discovered became clear (a colossal sculpture in the form of a city), they must have been stunned to silence, if not by the beauty of the work, then certainly by the sheer magnitude of human endeavor. What I felt that summer day on finding the stone, it, too, sacred and long forgotten, was similar, but not awe at a work of human creation. Instead, something closer to what might have been felt by the very first person to happen upon the boulder long ago, deep in a forest of much larger girth. A pause, a hesitation upon feeling that something was not normal. Not a feeling of foreboding but a sense that the place itself was extraordinary. The surface of the stone was roughly striated—not the usual granite boulder that is found in those hills—and the entire slope of the hill swelled outward at that point, the stone protruding from the crest of the rise. It appeared as if a fragment of the very core of the Earth had pushed to the surface and the land was bulging outward where its tip broke through the surface. Would the ancients need any other reasons to mark this place sacred?

Pushing through the brush to the uphill side of the stone, we found it possible to climb on top of the boulder. I sent my son up first and climbed up after him. Looking out from that perch above the treeline, the city spread out in the valley before us, a checkerboard of gray. The ancient stone our naze, we sat on the

edge of the Ice Age, looking out at a future already ours. A stream
of cars ran by below us amid the boxy apartment buildings and
powerlines. My son pointed excitedly at something, tugging at
my arm: a tower-crane shuttling precast-concrete panels up
from a truck at a construction site, from where we were, looking
just like a bright new toy. Sunlight glinted off the leaves surrounding us; the forest smelled hot. We each took another swig
of cool water. I padded pearls of sweat from my face; my son
headed back for the shaded side of the rock. The sun flared, the
city dissolved in waves of heat, leaving only brilliant rivers crossing open meadows.

The woods around the stone opened, filling with light. From
below came the sound of drumming, and a group of men dressed
in rough cloth came forward cautiously out of the shadows of the
trees, following each other in single file, their faces darkened by
rows of swirling tattoos. The drum, small and disk-shaped, like a
tambourine with a handle, was held by a woman whose hair flew
wildly about her shoulders, her neck and arms draped with jade
beads and bear claws. The men stopped as she approached the
edge of the open square, intensifying her beat. Encouraged, the
cicadas shrilled louder, their buzz rising and falling, at times dis-
sonant then peaking together unbearably loud. The drumming
stopped; the cicadas fell silent.

The woman knelt on the ground, touching it as if to sense
something, the way a mother feels the belly of a sick child. She
took some meadow grass from a satchel, bound it into a loose
knot, and placed it to her right, made another and set it to the
left. Rising, she turned to the first man in line, took from him a
small packet made of bamboo leaves, and carried it, arms out-

stretched, toward the base of the stone below us. I crouched down and crept to the edge, holding my breath, chest to stone, peering down at her as she set the packet down on the altar then turned and brought the other offerings forward, one by one: a handful of salt; branches laden with citrus fruit; a slain rabbit; a sheath of grains; a crude earthenware pot from which she sprinkled a milky liquid to anoint the offerings, the stone, and the land around it. The sweet scent of fermented grains rose on the warm air. A branch snapped behind me and I flipped over defensively but found only my son playing with some brittle twigs. He held one out to show me, then turned away. I looked back around but the shamanness and her men were gone. Above the treeline, rows of concrete boxes extended for miles to the south concealing the rivers. Some large leaves I hadn't noticed before lay scattered below on the altar.

We continued up the hill toward the overlook, leaving the sacred stone to its forest spirits. Arriving at our spot, we sat on an old pine that had fallen in a typhoon, dug out some sesame crackers and water, and enjoyed the snack in silence, scanning the city below. The high-pitched whir of a motor came intermittently on the breeze: a farmer cutting grass on the banks of his paddy, a shock of green hemmed in by roads and buildings. A last remaining fragment of the vast system of paddies that used to cover the entire valley, that still blanketed this part of Kyoto until a mere thirty years ago.

Rice. That was what drew the ancients away from the stone, allowed it to be forgotten and absorbed by the forest. As farming developed, the focus of life shifted away from the wild to the rice paddy, from hunting to village life. The stone was too far away, so to keep the gods closer to hand a shrine was built between the village and the mountain, as a link, a half-way point, between agricultural man and wild nature. A thousand years after that, but still a thousand years ago, a city was raised in the broad valley to the south; as it grew, it incorporated the village as an outlying neighborhood. The original shrine was moved several times and can now be found in a small forest some distance from where the sacred stone lies forgotten, gathering moss. At some point, the evergreen branch the villagers employed to carry the gods was replaced by a *mikoshi;* small at first—now the two-ton lacquered palanquin we struggled to move. A history several thousand years long, from forest oracle to village icon.

❀   ❀   ❀

This garden stone we are trying to haul today is much smaller than the sacred stone, yet still is somehow similar: something in the sandy hue and pitted texture of its surface, the way a small cleft runs down one side. A clump of moss still clings to it inhabited by a few busy ants, a microcosm of nature that we will bring into the garden unintentionally. Even as a stone in the garden represents an act of community—the farmer's mentality—so too, does it elicit the older sentiment of stones as links between man and the wild.

Back on our feet, we crouch once more, count and lift, shouldering the stone, taking measured steps around the last corner, onto the bare ground where the new garden will be. A few large trees remain from before, but otherwise the area has been cleared. We will begin making the garden with this stone; its placement will determine what comes after. In this we follow in the footsteps of the aristocrats who lived in this city a thousand years ago. They also built gardens at their residences, even though they had no word for gardening, simply the expression *ishi wo taten koto,* "the art of setting stones." Setting stones was so entirely fundamental to the act of garden building that it defined the process, and through the medium of the stone the designers of that era wove various meanings into their gardens. They set a stone and called it Shumisen, Japanese for Sumeru, the central mountain of Buddhist and Hindu cosmology; they set another and called it Fudō-myōō, the Buddhist deity who purges the world of evil; they set still another to evoke the image of a windswept ocean shore and express allegorically the waste and abject loneliness felt by lovers denied their love; and they set stones of specific colors around their home to balance the flow of life-energy based on rules of an ancient Chinese geomancy. The stones were animated with meanings potent and divers, and yet beyond all those cultural affections, they also remained a testimony to communal work and, deeper still, a symbolic link back to the wilderness. Beyond the superficial sculptural beauty of the stones and the great material value placed on them in later years, the ancient messages lay enfolded within them, informing all else, the way a primordial reptilian center remains at the stem of our brains.

With the end in sight, we find renewed energy and soon have the stone set roughly where it should be. I walk over to the house, remove my shoes on the large, flat-topped stone next to the veranda, and enter the newly built sitting room. The stone we set must be seen from the seat of honor, the place within the room where an esteemed guest will be entreated to sit, his back to the display alcove and face toward the garden. It is from there, seen through the frame created by the opening in the architecture, that the garden is best appreciated and so it is from there that the position of the first stone must be determined. The stone is almost right as it is, just slightly off balance. As I point to the left, the gardeners push in unison, tilting the stone slowly in that direction. The invisible line that passes down the center of the stone—like the one that ballet dancers are trained to sense within themselves to keep erect when pirouetting—falls in line with the downward flow of gravity and the stone suddenly acquires a presence, tangibly, as if someone important had just walked into view. The stone is set.

From here on, the placement of the other stones will follow the precedent of the first one. The ancient nobles wrote that this is the way gardens should be built, but they expressed it in another way, saying, "follow the request of the stone." Not, "balance the next stone with what was placed before," but "follow the *request* of the stone" because for them the stone was animate. It had desires, natural dispositions, *requests*, the fulfillment of which was essential to creating a well-balanced garden.

The stone in place, I move over to the veranda. Ten o'clock; time for a break. Tea is served by the woman of the house. The rich, nutty scent of buckwheat rises from the cup. The biscuits smell of cinnamon like the broken twigs at this morning's fire. The sky has cleared, the sun is now bright. Outside the garden wall, powerlines stretch between poles, black against the sky, a constant presence in Japan. Looking up at them, I remember a particular moment when carrying the *mikoshi*, wet with sweat and rain, pounding toward the shrine entrance. Shoulder thrust into the weight of the beam, head thrown back, I saw above us, beyond a frenzied blur of gilt ornaments, powerlines silhouetted against the night-lit sky. The lines formed an insanely tangled web, energized within by arrays of nuclear generators, pulsing silently, far away along the coast of the Japan Sea. The *mikoshi* surged, pressing into my neck. I responded along with those around me and it surged back, and then forward, moving powerfully yet naturally like a boat passing through a larger ship's wake. We danced that night beneath those wires, the organic communion of human power enacted under its more acute electric cousin. Which, I wonder now, is the more powerful, and which speaks more truly of us? Is it our social union—the strength of many backs together, the layering of mind on mind—that best describes us, or is it our technology, our intellect externalized and given form? In which do we see our future? Looking back into the garden, at the stone now set and rooted to its spot, I can't help but believe that long after the feverish engines that electrify and terrify us are made still and cold by a society more judicious than our own, the art of setting stones will remain, articulating the strength of our community and our immediacy to nature.

WINTERGREEN

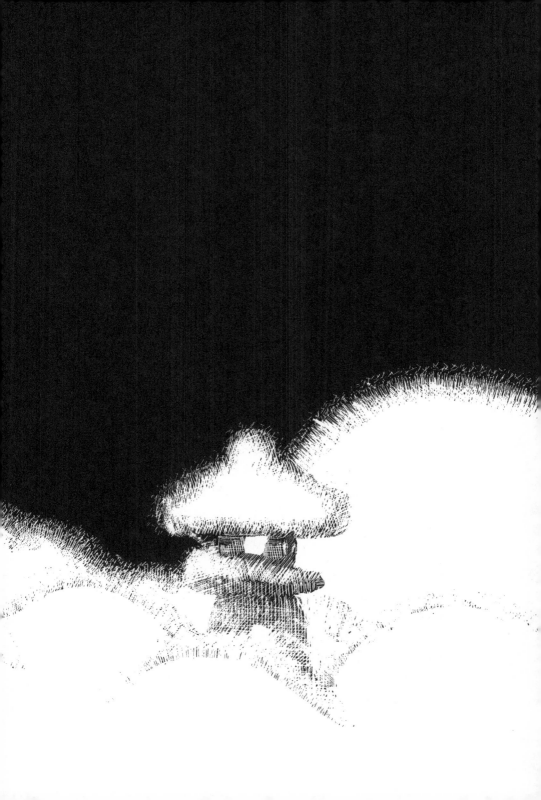

THINGS ARE NOT AS THEY SEEM. THE DEEPER ONE LOOKS, THE less so.

I've come to stay for a week at Yukio's place, house-sitting while he's away. For the past few days, most of my time has been spent in the garden: sweeping and pruning, sketching . . . looking deeper. In the evenings I watch the garden by moonlight, enthralled. Yesterday it began snowing heavily, and only in the last few hours has the storm begun to taper off. Tonight, the old house is dark, except for one room in which I've set some candles. They flicker in drafts and cast a restless pale light across the tatami and tan clay walls. The faltering light plays tricks with a carved Buddha that sits in the *tokonoma*. At times it seems perfectly serene and then, briefly, to be smiling. The room, too, seems to shift and bend with the vagaries of the light, contracting when the candle flares, expanding into darkness as it wanes. The candles flutter, sending pulses through the room; moods wash across the Buddha's face like surf on sand. What seemed so solid a few hours ago, sculpture and architecture, becomes now fluid, its reality not as fixed at night as it was by day.

In the garden, diffused moonlight falls on deep snowdrifts, luminous and soft. It's still snowing but lightly, falling slowly through the windless air, imparting to the room a mild sense of motion as it did during Chizuru's funeral, rising upward against the downward flow outside. It's time to ready the bath. I bundle up in a warm padded-cotton jacket and slide open the heavy wooden door that leads outside from the earth-floored kitchen. It seems brighter outside than in, the snow not so much reflecting light as emitting it, glowing like the night-wake of ships in phosphorescent seas. Snow gathers on my shoulders as I head along the path to the bathhouse.

On the side of the building, set low in one wall, is a small firebox that heats the tub inside, a cast-iron vessel shaped like half an egg, just large enough to hold one person squatting down. I grab a handful of twigs from a pile nearby and light them. The snow chills the back of my neck; the flames warm my face. When the twigs have caught, I push them further into the firebox and start adding sticks, one by one, until a hot fire is crackling away around the exposed bottom of the tub. Smoke rises from the chimney in gray spirals through falling snow. Smoke and snow, heat and cold; they swirl around each other, and the sharpness of the night air is mellowed by a welcome, woody scent. The fire set, I go back inside, brushing snow from my head and shoulders before stepping back into the dark stillness of the house.

141

A half hour later, candle in hand, I make my way to the bathhouse down an indoor corridor, moving in a flickering bubble of warm light. When I slide open the door a cloud of steam rolls out and wafts up to the ceiling, carrying with it the delightful scents of cypress and citrus. The *sunoko*, a slatted pallet in front of the bath that one sits on while washing, is new and still smells of freshly cut wood. In the bath float two *yuzu*, yellow citrus fruits shaped like small oranges but more richly aromatic. The scents mingle, woody and pungent, part forest, part field. I set the candle on a shelf by the bath, strip and squat, wash outside the bath first, rinse with hot water scooped from the tub, then slip into the water. Testing the heat tentatively—toe to ankle to knee— I ease down until only my head remains above the surface, hot water dabbing at my beard. The consuming heat penetrates, and after a momentary cringe and contraction, every muscle relaxes and releases into the heat. Just as salmon scent their way upstream to the specific place of their birth, this bath returns me

similarly, but not to the physical place, instead to a sensory equiv-
alent—warm, darkened, close, and safe—a place for reflection as
much as for cleansing, looking back to see ahead, turned within
to find what lies beyond.

Next to the bath is a long horizontal window. Yukio posi-
tioned it so that when opened it would offer a framed view of the
garden. I blow out the candle and sit in the dark for a while enjoying the heat and near-silence—the cedar-citrus smell, the lapping
sound of water at the edge of the tub—then slowly slide the window open. As if unscrolling a painting, the snow-covered garden
unfolds, pale rounded forms that swell and roll like breakers
across a reef, a night tide frozen in time. And like an ocean, although the complex play of the surface attracts the eye, it is its
hidden depths that compel the spirit. The shapes of the garden are
indistinct yet familiar, rounded hummocks where there used to
be clipped azaleas, pointed piles where stones had been, the gesture of a well-shaped pine but not its details. I know the garden
well; I've spent many quiet hours in the past few days sketching
the details concealed from me now. But if this had been my first
time, I wonder if I could have seen through the thick snow cover
and divined the real structure of the garden, or would it have appeared as only random shapes?

Beneath the snow, the garden remains alive in all its subtlety.
There is a bird's nest hidden safely inside an azalea. I know. I found
it once while pruning. Next to the azalea there is a rock with three
long notches in its side that catch rain and guide it down like a
waterfall. I have seen that, too, and dreamed it a landscape. There
are buds by the hundred on a camellia by the veranda that will ease
open one by one in spring when no one is looking. These things I

know but can imagine more: some downy feathers in the nest pressed tightly by the weight of the snow; a spider bound in its own silk burrowed deep within one of the notches of the rock, tucked in tight against the winter cold; a faint flow of sap wending its way through countless hollow woody cells. Fungal nets prob-ing the soil; pale-white cicada larvae curled tightly in the frozen ground, feeding on sap, their tubular hearts beating on the thought of spring; green moss glistening in the crystalline light. The garden lies hidden, obscured by winter, yet remains tremu-lous and live, intricate and abundant in countless recesses. Spring will pull back the cover and reveal it again, but somehow I prefer it as it is, merely a suggestion of a garden; all margin and innuen-do. It solicits inquiry; encourages imagining of what lies within.

143

In elementary school, we were given an experiment, a les-son in visualizing the inner workings of things. Each student got a box, flat as a pie box, made sturdily of wood. The boxes had han-dles and knobs sticking out from their narrow sides, each painted a different, bright color. The idea behind the experiment was to play with the handles and come up with an explanation for the mechanism inside the box that connected them. If you twisted a yellow knob, for instance, a green lever on the other side would go up and down rhythmically and, at the same time, a red dowel would pump in and out of the box like a piston. Move the green lever up and down, however, and though the red piston would still pump the yellow knob wouldn't budge. There were other clues as well, sounds associated with movements, a rasping or whirring or thud, and the touch of the handles themselves, vibra-tions tracing silently through our fingertips.

After we had fiddled with the boxes for a half hour or so, we were asked to make sketches of what was going on inside—to make a guess based on what we saw and felt as to what mechanism could explain all the interrelated movements of the various handles. Papers began filling with gears and cables and fulcrumed levers, springs and strings and sawlike rasps. When all the students had sketched out their own versions of the inner workings of their boxes, we opened the lids, and compared theory with reality. What remains with me today about the lesson is that even though some of our plans correctly explained the handles' movements, they mostly didn't match what we found inside the boxes at all. The real lesson was becoming aware of the gap between theory and truth.

We want to know the truth, so we open things and potter in their innards hoping to find out what makes them work. We take apart our world and lay it flayed and raw on the board. We probe beneath its surfaces hoping to discover not just what *could be* but what *is*.

Yet partial knowledge, though flawed, can be frighteningly powerful. In the 1940s, the array of subatomic particles described by high-energy physics was simplistic in scope compared to the pantheon proposed today. Decades would pass before quarks, now held to be among the most elementary particles, would be hypothesized let alone observed. Yet on July 16, 1945, the desert at Alamogordo, New Mexico shook with thunder and light, howling in a maelstrom of gritty wind, and later that summer, so too Hiroshima and Nagasaki.

The wind gusts, carrying aloft falling snow. The delicate flakes rise as easily as they fall, tumbling, crystalline and glittery, tracing sparkling eddies through the air. Nothing gets pinned down; not snow, not atoms. The essence of that thought is contained in the Heisenberg uncertainty principle, which states that it is impossible to know both the position and velocity of a subatomic particle with accuracy—what we know of one disrupts an understanding of the other. It's not that we need finer equipment; the observation itself is the problem. At that level, perceiving the world physically modulates it; the act of viewing changes what is seen. The fundamental building blocks of all things— which we once believed to be fixed and solid and unequivocally real—turn out to be timorous things turning and hiding at no more than a glance.

145

The stone enfolding the spider is granite; what greater emblem of solidity is there? But break it down. Granite is mainly composed of quartz, quartz of oxygen, and oxygen . . . of nothing, mainly. In fact, the whole crust of the Earth is mainly oxygen; the planet, like the rock, is mainly nothing. Insects, of course, are no more substantial, so out there in the winter garden lies the enigma of a spider-shaped void abiding safely in a crevice of rock-shaped emptiness. Look too closely and firmament turns fluid. Stone sublimates into a vaporous field of energy, no more subject to our tenure than the glint off falling snow.

If the world is unascertainable at the level of the fantastically small, it is no less so where it lies at arm's reach. Whatever its ultimate true form is, we don't know it. What comes to us does so indirectly, through the filters of our senses. Unlike one-celled creatures, we are not directly socketed to our environment and so are inherently incapable of primary understanding. Our senses filter out the extremes; all we are left to mull is a narrow band somewhere in the middle.

What's more, our intellect, the very tool we use to probe, prejudices our vision with its history, an encoding that begins at birth, if not before, in the bathlike warmth of the uterus even as our embryonic cells split and fold. What we perceive as physical reality is no more than a mental construct, scenes that are colored, scented, and shaped, and given cadence and meaning, by the clockwork of our physiologies. We go blank into no experience, are never the empty vessel waiting to receive. Not without training that is (or untraining, perhaps)—convincing the mind not to be aware of itself.

Philosophic and mystic traditions of perceiving the world as illusion run deep in many cultures. In Ecclesiastes we find the Speaker saying, "emptiness, emptiness . . . all is empty." Jean-Paul Sartre comments in *Nausea* that "things are entirely what they appear to be and behind them . . . there is nothing." Hindus call this illusion, or self-delusion, *maya,* a word that still carries the aura of its ancient meaning of being under a magical spell. For Zen Buddhists, "form is emptiness," *shikizoku zekū.* But, interestingly, they also turn it around. "Emptiness is form," they say, *kūsoku zeshiki,* a thought found in the Wisdom sutras. Despite the fact that all is in flux and thus "empty" of a permanent form, emptiness is the inherent nature of matter and thus indivisible from it. One is the other. There is no difference.

I nudge the *yuzu;* it bobs and turns, slender leaves rolling in and out of the water, here again, gone again, complex reflections flickering across ripples on the water surface. I've seen this before, in a garden of an old townhouse I visited once long ago. There was a *yuzu* set on the edge of a stone water basin, struck full by sunlight: a bright yellow orb and five slim leaves hanging close to the water surface. It appeared in triplicate: the fruit itself, its reflection on the water surface, and a shadow cast through the clear water onto the bottom of the water basin. Three images, but which one real? Touch the fruit; it's stippled skin is cool. Pick it up, feel its weight. Squeeze it; the scent tingles, making you breathe deep and slow, nostrils flaring. It's undeniably real. But look more closely. Probe it down to the smallest possible level, and what will you get? Atoms? Electrons? Not even that. According to superstring theory, the latest postulation by nuclear physicists investigating the micro universe, all you'll find at the most fundamental level are infinitesimally small, one-dimensional oscillating strings. The pitch of the oscillation determines the type of matter the string produces. An electron is one tone, a proton another. Our world is, the theory hypothesizes, at its most fundamental level, simply vibrations. The phenomenal, tangible world we sense around us (that we are so convinced is solid and real) is no more than ripples cast up into the larger dimension we inhabit. Is reality the fruit, the reflection, or the shadow?

We think of nature in three dimensions, but physicists propose more, many more. At every point within the familiar three, they posit at least seven new dimensions; each point in space is twisted around itself like a knotted vine. Things exist, they say, in all those dimensions at once; things slide through them all simultaneously with each movement, unknowingly. The process is too minute to register, but were we able to look closely enough, the moving world would appear to ripple, like *yuzu* leaves reflected on the surface of the bath.

We need not take the notions of string theory and ten-dimensional space on face value. They are only theories that are being taken into the general canon because they solve certain enigmas that were heretofore unexplained. Undoubtedly they'll be replaced by new theories at a later date. No one is saying, "this is how things really are," that there are little strings inside of electrons if you look real closely. No one has looked inside the box. They're only saying that if you explain that level of the micro universe in terms of strings, the mathematics begin to work, and previously disparate theorems becomes synchronous. In particular, general relativity (an explanation of gravity related to things extremely large and massive) and quantum mechanics (an explanation of other forces related to subatomic particles), two theories that were formerly at odds, now can be seen to flow naturally from the same theory. Whether strings are the ultimate solution is not the point. The theory reaffirms what mystics have been saying for thousands of years: if you look deeply, things are not as they seem. So much depends on where you set your focus.

Beneath the crystalline snow is a bed of velvet moss still green; below the moss, the plump white curve of a cicada larva nestled in dark soil; within the curve a muscle beating dimly; at the center of the muscle a blood cell, spinning; within the cell an atom of oxygen, and at the core of that atom a string, quivering. Hunker down and listen; it sounds like a bow plucked, like waves washing through pebbles on a shore, like the hiss and crackle of a universe just born. The hiss becomes a hum, the hum a low-voiced chant—a prayer intoned in a darkened hall by black-robed monks. They chant because it is regenerative and healing; the words they use just meaningless shells, the content residing in the tone itself. The chant reverberates in mesmerizing harmonics, repeating in cyclic riffs until it becomes a pulse, steady and warm, drumming close within their chests. Outside the hall snow falls, blanketing everything.

The chanting monks are Buddhist, a religion that developed out of the context of Hinduism. One aspect of Buddhist teaching that set it apart from the older Hindu practice was its disbelief in the existence of a fixed soul, *atman*. Hindu practice centered on a belief in individual souls and a greater, pure soul, called *brahman*, the ideal being the alignment of lesser to greater, the synchrony of *atman* with *brahman*. Buddhists took a different point of view. They looked at the world and saw only flux—all things at all times in an ongoing process of change—and concluded that in a world that knows no stillness, nothing could be fixed, not even souls. They divined the essence of change from the landscape, looking at shifting weather patterns, flowing rivers, cycles of life and death, all the aspects of nature that speak of impermanence. We confirm that vision by cleaving the landscape, piercing beyond what can be seen to the very brink of existence, and finding there no more than a hum.

Mystics also describe the essence of life as a vibration. Their asceticisms are intended to allow them a direct understanding of that basic energy and to force them out of three dimensions into many, where the quake and thrum of nature lies free and apparent. The parallels with string theory (in concept, not application) are remarkable. Some say that's not surprising, that physicists and mystics, after all, are only human and so are capable of conceiving only things within the scope of human experience. Still, however limiting the human scope may be, the potential of our imagery is yet vast, and the idea that the mystic path and the scientific one end at the same shore is both humbling and reas-

149

suring, an intimation that knowledge is approachable from many angles.

The wind picks up and a flurry of snow comes in through the open window, swirls into the rising steam, settles to the bath and melts. Water, steam, and snow. I inhabit a triptych of H_2O. Random flakes cling to the edges of the bath and the window sill. Looking closer at the window pane, I find a few crystals illuminated softly from behind, glowing translucent white. Some are star-shaped, some platelike, all six-sided, an aspect inherent to snowflakes because of the shape and bonding patterns of water molecules. Micro revealed in macro. And yet, there is nothing "snowy" about a cold water molecule. Micro denying macro; a primal contradiction. At the atomic level, the stuff of which our world is made is entirely unlike our perception of the world itself. Yet, when micro multiplies to macro it does so in a way so closely prescribed by its nature that the larger object becomes an exact reflection of the parts comprised within. Not *like* them, but entirely *of* them—*kūsoku zeshiki*, emptiness is form; there is no difference.

The basic stuff of the world is ephemeral beyond belief, existing without color or scent or constancy in time or space. Yet put billions of those apparitions together and, somehow, they generate our world: a curved white larva; a snowy garden; a man in a tub. It's unbelievable. It would be no more remarkable if the glitter of the falling snow were to suddenly congeal and bring forth gifts; tai chi dancers, lotuses blooming, the face of Buddha, smiling.

❋   ❋   ❋

I ease down into the warmth of the tub and splash some water on my face to wash away beads of sweat. Laying my head back, I gaze up into the darkness and watch steam gather below the ceiling like clouds—like clouds I saw through trees, laying back in a similar way on a crisp day this past autumn. The maples were brilliant, a shade of fire-red that denied its botanical origins. The leaves were just at their peak and were beginning to fall. Each time the wind picked up, armfuls would scatter to the ground. I laid back, looking up at the tree silhouetted against the clouds, enjoying the gentle cascade of leaves.

Above the maple was a pine tree, its rich green needles a luxuriant backdrop. The branches of the pine and maple overlapped in places forming a woven pattern of green and red. In another week, all the leaves of the maple would be gone. Winter would settle in; snow would blanket the ground. But the pine, its leaves rolled tightly into needles to prevent damage from winter expiration, would remain green. Both trees, maple and pine, evolved in response to their environments: different solutions, both equally effective. From where I lay, the layering of the two read like a *mandala*, an icon rendering clear a deeper truth. Each tree elegantly designed, each beautiful in its own right, yet different, making visible the consequences of botanical evolution. Deciduous and evergreen—the image of the two so closely overlapped revealed at a glance the diverse economy of nature. Apprehending truth, I saw, lies not only in choosing *what* to look at but *how* to look at it. When seen from the right angle the world speaks with outstanding clarity. All one needs to do is change one's perspective, view the ordinary anew. Some go to great lengths to do that, like the marathon monks.

Northeast of Kyoto a mountain called Hiei-zan sits prominently above the city. It has featured in the religious and geoman-
tic landscape of the valley since before the imperial city was
founded here twelve hundred years ago. In a deep cryptomeria
forest that shades its summit is Enryakuji, a sprawling temple of
the Tendai sect of Buddhism. Every so often, one of its monks ac-
complishes a feat of physical endurance that verges on impossible,
and through that extremity entirely shifts his perspective, evicting
self-awareness from his mind. The ritual is a thousand-day pil-
grimage that, despite its length, never takes him past the limits of
the surrounding valley; the journey is intensely physical but focused on gaining ground within the spirit, not outward in space.
Each night the monk runs down the mountain on a forty-kilome-
ter loop through Kyoto, returning to the summit at dawn for
prayers, chores, and rest. As time goes by, the pace and pitch in-
tensify, culminating in the *doiri*, a nine-day sleepless fast that
brings him to the brink of death, starved and utterly spent. When
it's all over, if he has lasted, if he's alive (for some have died), at-
tendants will help him out of the dark prayer hall into the soft
light of the forest. Exhausted yet energized, wavering on the thin
edge of life, he beholds the world anew as if with newborn eyes:
fragile, yearning to begin.

There are times when asceticism leads to enlightenment,
and there are times when epiphanies happen with far less struggle, sometimes by just seeing things from a new angle. Lie down
and watch trees overlap and find that they describe in the subtleties of their forms the history of their species. Sit in a bath and
see a winter garden through a narrow window, and in the frame
(and *because* of the framing) watch the garden turn from place to

painting. In the new perspective allowed by that shifting reality—
by seeing nature metamorphose to art—the original, once understood and familiar, is seen anew and rediscovered.

As I climb out of the bath, a cloud of steam lifts from my
body into the cold air as if I were evaporating. I slip on a robe and
fumble my way dreamily back to the room with the carved Buddha. Ready for sleep, I lay out a futon and blow out all the candles
except one that I set by the head of the quilts as I slip into them,
swaddled and content. I jot a few last thoughts down in a note-
book and put out the last light. A black tide flows into the room,
filling everything, floor to ceiling. It pours into the *tokonoma* and
cloaks the Buddha, which disappears then re-emerges, tinged
with moonlight.

It is thought that the origins of the *tokonoma* were spaces in
ancient homes left empty for gods to descend into. The form we
know today, though, developed later, during the sixteenth century, as part of tiny rustic tea houses. The intent of tea gatherings
held in those spartan buildings was to change the mindset of the
people who participated, to heighten their perceptions by placing
them in a rarefied space whose simplicity would increase their
awareness of subtleties and encourage them to focus more intently at all levels. Share a bowl of tea, appreciate art, see things as
they are. The process was straightforward—simplify to accentu-
ate—and the *tokonoma* was an essential part. A space set aside ex-
clusively for displaying works of art within a room already
preciously small, it focused attention on whatever was placed
within it by holding it apart, the way altars sanctify objects by el-
evating them. Gardens do the same for nature.

A garden is a piece of nature held apart to bring it into

focus. Gardens heighten nature's wild language by simplifying it, by sieving its complex messages to extract choice kernels: a subtle flow of time; a boundary that is and yet isn't; a balance born of imbalances. We amplify nature's messages when we build a garden and in turn the garden awakens us with those thoughts. Sitting and reflecting, drawn into the garden and out of ourselves, we find we are aware of familiar things in ways we weren't before, granted, if only for a brief moment, newborn eyes.

154

The snow has all but stopped; the only sound is my own breathing. Moonlight reflects from the garden, tinting my hands silver, wizening the Buddha's face. I close my eyes and imagine spring, force it into motion. The cover of snow lifts suddenly from the garden like a plaster cast. The cicada stirs and wriggles out of the ground to mount the nearest tree, carrying aloft the sound of waves beating in its heart. Sap wells up from fungal nets to emergent leaves in a rush of unseen hydraulics. A hundred red camellia blossoms gush at once and blow, falling in full bloom like dabs of blood on moss.

The dream recedes; outside the shell of the garden is mute, but not its heart. Though it cannot be seen, wintergreen lies shallow beneath the snow. Imagining it is an act of faith, and one of hope. If the garden holds its secrets close for a while, it will offer them in time. I can wait. I must. For the garden is an ocean that surrenders its mysteries only to the abiding, casts them up for only the watchful to find. If you come to a garden, it will not disappoint, but you must come as to an ocean, ready to explore, curious, in awe, tuned to waves, dreamy yet alert. Give me a garden to sit by, and I will attend it by the hour. Give me but bare ground and I will build one, and keep vigil upon its quiet shores.

Printed in the USA
CPSIA information can be obtained
at www.ICGtesting.com
JSHW060143191124
73809JS00002B/3